BEYOND THE TUNNEL OF HISTORY

Beyond the Tunnel of History

Jacques Darras

with

Daniel Snowman

Ann Arbor
The University of Michigan Press

Copyright © 1990 by Jacques Darras and Daniel Snowman

First published by the University of Michigan Press 1990

Published in the United States of America by
The University of Michigan Press

1993   1992   1991   1990   4   3   2   1

Library of Congress Cataloguing-in-Publication Data
Darras, Jacques, 1939–
   Beyond the tunnel of history/Jacques Darras with Daniel Snowman.
      p.   cm.
   A rev. and expanded version of the 1989 BBC Reith lectures given
   by Darras at the University of Picardy in France.
   ISBN 0–472–10208–7
   1. Great Britain–Relations–France.   2. Great Britain–
   Civilization–French influences.   3. France–Civilization–British
   influences.   4. France–Relations–Great Britain.   I. Snowman,
   Daniel.   II. Title
   DA47.1.D33   1990
   303.48′241044–dc20   90–34702

Printed in Great Britain

Contents

List of Plates

Introduction

'The emergence of polyphony was the aesthetic equivalent of the development of democracy.' Jacques Darras dropped this remark casually over lunch one day. It was a provocative comment, of course, doubtless overstated, and not intended for public consumption. But when I challenged him he spoke lovingly of the music of Dufay and Josquin, the canvases of the Van Eycks and the political benevolence of Duke Philip the Good of Burgundy. I think this was the moment when in my mind at least I felt that this man had to be the 1989 BBC Reith Lecturer.

In the past, the Reith Lectures have usually been given by a distinguished British (or at least native-English-speaking) academic reading from carefully honed scripts. It is a difficult brief. The Reith Lectures, given annually since 1947, are the most prestigious event on BBC Radio, a programme project for which the invitation comes, via the Director-General, from the Board of Governors. To do full justice to the occasion the Lecturer must somehow find a tone and style that will engage a radio audience, while at the same time creating a new intellectual construct that will outlive the broadcasts themselves. Some of the most original pieces of writing for the Lectures have been virtually incomprehensible to the ear at a single hearing; some of the most engaging broadcasts merely re-hashes of material already familiar. An outstanding few Lecturers have managed to sail triumphantly between Scylla and Charybdis: George Kennan ('Russia, the Atom and the West') in 1957, G.M. Carstairs ('This Island Now') in 1962, Edmund Leach ('A Runaway World?') in 1967, and Geoffrey Hosking on the USSR in 1988.

During the early discussions about the 1989 Reith Lectures, I suggested that we break with tradition and find a French Lecturer (or Lectrice). Not necessarily a historian to talk about the French Revolution, I said; we would probably still be suffering from Revolutionary indigestion by the time the Lectures were on the air, four months after the Bicentenary had come and gone. Rather, we should try to find someone who could take the Bicentenary as a starting point, discuss the uses and abuses of history, take a fresh look at the myths that shroud the mutual perceptions of the British and French, and go on to suggest other ways of looking at the past if we are to live harmoniously together in the new Europe that beckons.

Nice idea, they said. Now find your Lecturer. So I went to France on a secret mission, meeting in the course of my travels a number of fascinating French men and women (some of whom I recorded for a series called 'Encounters in France' which was broadcast on Radio Four in June and July 1989 during the run-up to the Bicentenary). It was on this trip that I first met Jacques Darras.

On that occasion we talked of many things, but the Reith Lectures were not among them. He told me of his poetry, his love of 'northernness', and his preference for the expressive pan-European culture of the High Middle Ages rather than the over-refined Enlightenment of the eighteenth century or the often brutal nationalisms of the nineteenth and twentieth. Whatever the quality of Darras's poetry (which I had yet to read) or of his history (which he invoked in a way professionals might have found selective), there was no doubting his intellectual vigour and the wit, the brilliance and the conviction of his conversation. Here was a communicator of the top rank, a real Ancient Mariner whose spell was inescapable; and who was able to cast it, moreover, in powerful, idiomatic English.

I reported back to my BBC colleagues. The year would see not only the Bicentenary of the French Revolution but also the centenary of the birth of the Founding Father of the BBC, John Reith, after whom the Lectures were named. We owed it to Reith, I thought, in this of all years not to broadcast a dull set of Lectures. Why ask Jacques Darras to write and read a set of Lectures in what is to him a foreign language? This I felt could stilt his style. Instead, I suggested we break precedent further and encourage Darras to talk freely from notes. He and I would keep closely in touch over all the preliminary work and I would have a detailed knowledge of the shape and content of each Lecture before we recorded it. But when we got to the studio sessions, we would not think of them as a means of 'capturing' the thoughts of this year's Lecturer; instead, I would encourage Jacques to approach the studio as an opportunity to fly, to liberate the poet in him, to talk freely to his listeners as he had talked to me that first time we met.

The BBC is often portrayed as enmeshed in tradition and red tape and the Reith Lectures are I suppose the programmes most deeply imbued with the Corporation's spirit. But I must report that my proposals for a novel approach received total support. 'You are pushing at an open door as far as I am concerned', said Radio Three Controller John Drummond when I first told him of my idea of a series of Reith Lectures spoken freely from notes. Michael Green, Controller of Radio Four, was equally encouraging. I suggested that we precede the series with a stereophonic radio feature in which I would coax Jacques Darras to reveal himself during visits to locations that had played an important part in his intellectual autobiography. This too was accepted.

*   *   *   *   *

As Jacques Darras and I worked and travelled together during the first half of 1989, I learned more about the man and the ideas he hoped to communicate in the Lectures. He is a poet, writer, translator and academic with a passion for the English language and capable of using it with a degree of creative energy that puts many native speakers to shame. Anyone who translates Walt Whitman and Ezra Pound, David Jones and Basil Bunting into French is a linguistic risk-taker and Darras's conversation, like his own writing, is peppered with wit, allusion and *double entendre*. 'Beware! Plant Crossing!' said a notice alongside roadworks he and I drove past one day. I feebly pretended to indicate a curbside flower looking left, right and left again. 'Must be a creeper!' riposted Jacques crisply. And he emitted a positively Rabelasian guffaw at my report of a BBC colleague who, on seeing a notice of Jacques's 1988 book *Le Génie du Nord*, thought the title referred to the author.

'Northernness' is certainly one of the motors that drives Jacques Darras. Born in northern France not far from the Channel, he first learned his English in Scotland and has a love of Celtic art and Flemish architecture, long shadows, thick clouds, heavy cakes and rich autumnal colours quite uncharacteristic of most French intellectuals. During the preparation of the Reith Lectures, Jacques and I travelled to Artois and to Picardy: to the village where he was born in 1939; to the picturesque city of Laon, a 'City of Light' during the Dark Ages; and to the acres of war graves commemorating the mindless massacres of the First World War. We visited Brussels and, in particular, the Grote Markt or Grand-Place that was later to feature so prominently in the first Lecture. And we travelled across to the highlands and islands of Scotland, a region and a culture which still figure powerfully in his imagination. *Le Génie du Nord* contains an almost mystical chapter on the light of Iona.

The first time Jacques and I sat down to go through the Reith Lectures in detail was in fact on the sands of Iona one bright morning in May. On this rocky little outpost, once the seat of Celtic Christianity, we talked of St Columba and of Robert Burns, of heroism and failure, and of the destructive passions of Louis XIV and Napoleon. It was here that Jacques spelled out to me his poetic idea of linking the physicality of the Grand-Place in Brussels to the development of democracy. By the time we arrived back at our hotel several hours later, windswept, sand on our heels and our faces showing early signs of a tan, the first Lecture was all but ready for broadcasting and the second well down the slipway. I remember wondering whether I would be able to tap the same visionary imagination that had flowed so freely as we talked on the sands of Iona when we came to record these first two Lectures in Paris a few weeks later. In the event I think we did. The spirit of St Columba stayed with us.

*　　　*　　　*　　　*　　　*

In addition to his love of the North, much of Darras's thinking is coloured by his passion for the life and culture of the Middle Ages. In Laon he led me to documents dating from the time of Charlemagne and showed how, here at least, the so-called 'Dark Ages' were really a pinnacle of enlightenment. In Arras and Brussels his attention was caught by the great achievements of the Duchy of Burgundy. Everywhere he spoke about language itself. 'A profound impoverishment of the French language set in,' he says disdainfully, 'with the establishment in 1635 by Richelieu of the Académie Française which squeezed the language into a corset from which it has never escaped.' By elevating the French language to quasi-official status, he argues, it became more refined, rather like white sugar or white bread with the 'guts' removed. There is of course plenty of fine French poetry and prose, and a tradition of elegant letter-writing. But try reading most modern French literature aloud, says Darras, let alone those arcane letters with their fancy-formula endings, and the excessively polished sophistication of the language will often render the meaning so subtle as to remain essentially uncommunicated.

In late Medieval times, on the contrary, the emerging French language was 'full of juice, full of flavour', an integral product of the society that used it, rough, rugged, robust, raunchy and expressive. When poets spoke, they did so out loud; people listened and even joined in. For what was a poet but a street singer, a story teller, a newscaster, a kind of sound stage for the wider society of which he was part? Poets did not write to be read in reverential silence by other poets, academics or reviewers. They spoke, and sang, and laughed and shouted and cried out loud: they provided the voice of Everyman. At that period, moreover, the poet crossed cultural boundaries. National and lingusitic frontiers had not yet hardened, says Darras, and scholars and singers moved with ease from Oxford to Paris to Heidelberg to Padua, sharing and spreading an essentially pan-European culture that we are only now on the verge of recapturing six or seven centuries later.

All this makes Jacques Darras something of an outsider in his own country. The French traditionally like their culture national, and prefer their artists and thinkers to gravitate towards straight lines, clear skies and explicit literary and political doctrines expressed in carefully refined language. Yet here is a Frenchman whose heart yearns for the rough, the curvilinear, the implicit, the imprecise, the uncertain, the impermanent, the inconsistent; above all, for the militantly multi-cultural.

The Darras heart is kept reasonably hidden within the sleeve. He is after all a northerner, somewhat formal, the passions no less intense for being interior. But, like the Celtic poets he admires so much — James Joyce, David Jones, Hugh McDiarmid, Brendan Behan, Dylan Thomas — he is a man whose intense love of language, ours as well as his own, pours forth in creative torrents when tapped. Spurred on by his love of a rich Rabelaisian culture he feels we have a chance to revive, Jacques Darras writes poetry to be read aloud and has a growing reputation in France and abroad for his readings of his own and other people's poetry. There is a consistency, a continuum between his art and his life, a sense of mission to language and the spoken word, and a desire to use language — languages — as his way of contributing to the multi-cultural Europe that he feels is developing alongside the progress of the Common Market.

*   *   *   *   *

As work on the 1989 Reith Lectures progressed, Jacques Darras and I were keenly aware that the context in which they would be received was shifting radically and almost daily. From the outset we had agreed that Jacques would focus on the multi-layered historical and cultural connections between France and Britain, and suggest how we might build on these as we move towards an increasingly united Europe. Gradually his main themes emerged: the civic square as a rallying point for political aspirations, cross-frontier mobility as a yardstick of genuine freedom, the excitements and dangers of romantic nationalism, the ambivalence of the French towards their German-Gothic origins. As the time approached for the talks to be broadcast, however, Jacques and I, like everyone else, became gripped by dramatic events in the communist world — where, incredibly, many of these very themes were being given unforgettably tangible form. No city square embodied its people's hunger for democracy more poignantly than Tiananmen — or more joyously than Wenceslas

Square in Prague; the iron curtain was torn apart in Hungary and (even more spectacularly) in Berlin, allowing literally millions of people a mobility none had ever dreamed of achieving; resurgent nationalism shook the Soviet Union in Armenia, Moldavia, the Baltic states and elsewhere, while further west the spectre of German unification stirred once more.

Mr Gorbachev's 'Common European Home', at first regarded as little more than rhetoric, rapidly came to acquire a variety of possible interpretations as European leaders and commentators in East and West alike struggled to keep abreast of events. Clutching for historical parallels, some recalled the liberation of Europe from Nazi thraldom in 1944–5. Others talked of the downfall of the Soviet empire and suggested dark analogies with Austro-Hungary in the years preceding August 1914. Wasn't 1989 *really* more like 1848, asked some? Or 1789? Such questions, with their attendant hopes and fears, were unavoidable in those heady days and weeks as one communist regime after another desperately tried to deal with the mounting antagonism of its own populace. Instinctively, as events galloped headlong into an unknown future, people sought lessons, and perhaps refuge, from the past.

Thus a major achievement of the 1989 Reith Lectures, I think, was to help provide the deeper historical and cultural background to current events for which people were thirsting. They knew about Hitler, Stalin, NATO, the Warsaw Pact and the invasions of Hungary in 1956 and Czechoslovakia in 1968. But the 'tunnel of history' offered by Jacques Darras helped lead people much deeper into European history and myth. His Reith Lectures thus proved to be an astonishingly timely attempt to cast light on the newly emerging Europe of tomorrow by observing it through the colourful prism of its past.

*   *   *   *   *

The memorable year 1989 marked, as I have mentioned, not only the Bicentenary of the French Revolution but also the centenary of the birth of Lord Reith, another somewhat formal northerner not afraid to use the media for the communication of messages in which he profoundly believed. I do not know what Reith would have thought of Jacques Darras's attempt to refashion British and French cultural history in the light of 1992 and beyond, and I suspect he might have balked at the almost volcanic force of some of Darras's unscripted narrations. But he would surely have admired Darras's commitment, his obvious integrity, the immense learning that underpinned all the talks, and Darras's sheer intellectual and verbal energy as he held together an argument that traversed several disciplines and a thousand years of multi-national history.

Normally, the texts of the Reith Lectures need little editing or adaptation for publication. This time, however, the process has inevitably been different. Each of the 1989 Reith Lectures was delivered in a great burst of imaginative energy and recorded (in a variety of studios in Paris and London) in what was usually a single take. Pernickity listeners were doubtless able to pick out the occasional minor imperfection: the slight mispronunciation or grammatical solecism. But Darras in full flight has something of the élan of a great musical risk-runner: Artur Rubinstein, say, or Leonard Bernstein. The Lectures were, to change metaphor, something of an intellectual high-wire act, never 'safe' or dull. How could this kind of explosive performance be adequately transferred to the printed page? Literal, word-for-word transcripts would clearly not do. Apart from any other considerations, some of what Jacques would have wished to say could not appear in broadcasts that had to be rigorously edited to fill a timed slot.

What I did, in fact, was to go back to our original uncut tapes and to the recordings made during our travels together and, starting from these, re-write the Lectures for publication. Jacques then drafted a number of extra chapters elaborating on ideas that he and I had discussed but which never found their way into the Lectures themselves; these too I refashioned into the fluent English that inevitably comes more easily to a native speaker. Thus the text of this book and any verbal or linguistic infelicities it may contain are basically mine: the ideas are essentially those of Jacques Darras. However, the division of labour is not quite as clear cut as this might imply since much of Jacques's original language remains. In particular, I have tried to retain his love of the sound of English and the freshness of his word-play; 'sharing and shearing' and 'bubbling, babbling Babel' for instance, are his. And for my part, I like to think that some of Jacques's ideas have been further sharpened in the course of our many working sessions together, and also of course by the further discipline inherent in having to produce publishable text.

The result, I hope, is a book that satisfactorily reproduces on the page in more substantial form one of the most stimulating and engaging series of Reith Lectures by a man who is a poet, professor, historian, citizen of Europe and, like all good poets, something of a seer.

December 1989   DANIEL SNOWMAN

1

Première Place

I live in Paris just by that vast grassy square, the Champ de Mars, almost in the shadow of the colossal iron structure that dominates it, the Eiffel Tower. And it came as a surprise (not only to me but, I suspect, to a lot of Parisians) to be reminded in the spring of our Bicentenary year, 1989, that the Eiffel Tower was built to mark the Centenary of the French Revolution; that is, just over a hundred years ago, in 1889. For the French, the Eiffel Tower is primarily a symbol of Paris, of the popularity of Paris and of France all over the world; it is the very image of France to the millions of tourists who flock here. It is also the place from which our first radio programmes were broadcast and is still one of our principal transmission centres. So perhaps the Eiffel Tower in 1989 was a fitting symbol with which to mark not only the French Revolution but also the centenary of the birth of John Reith. And the Champ de Mars, as we shall see, certainly embodies messages from history that we might wish to heed today.

The year 1989 was not in itself a particularly crucial one for celebration. Most French citizens were already more aware of the importance of 1992 and 1993, which are supposed to mark the emergence of a truly united Europe as such and the elimination of barriers between France and its our neighbours. To many, this is an exciting prospect, even though the magic moment at which 1992 becomes 1993 will not, of course, witness any sudden and spectacular elimination of national cultures or ways of thinking. Such things shift slowly, imperceptibly, and existing patterns of thought and behaviour will in any case have much to offer in the post-1992 pan-European world we will allegedly be inhabiting. To many French citizens,

11

indeed, the idea of '1992' represents less a promise than a threat, and the 'elimination of barriers' sounds ominous, even rather disquieting, as though some sort of knife — a guillotine perhaps — were being sharpened above our innocent French heads. If we wish to be in the anniversary business at all, it may be worth remembering that the High Noon of the Guillotine occurred not in 1789, but in 1792 and 1793.

As we approach, for better or for worse, the shared destiny of an increasingly united Europe, and as the British and French in particular finally learn to jettison a thousand years of mutual suspicion and animosity with the building of the Channel Tunnel, I want to tunnel back through our history and suggest that our respective national pasts will need to be reinterpreted in the light of a shared future. Victor Hugo said of the French Revolution that it was a monument not to the past but to the future, an event more important for what it presaged than for what it ended. In the same way, the monument I want to begin to erect is intended to be more a marker for the future than a commemoration of the past. The two are inextricably interrelated, of course. A milestone tells you both how far you have come and how far you still have to go. And in order to suggest ways of facing the future, I will have much to say above the ways in which we regard, and often disregard and misregard, our past. In doing so I would like to invite you to join me on a tour of my personal European Museum. As we travel through the tunnel of history together, we will call upon philosophy, history and poetry as we start to reshape and rewrite our common cultural heritage, and consider and occasionally reconstruct the great landmarks and symbols of our past.

Where should we start our journey? Not perhaps with the French Revolution or its Centenary or even its Bicentenary. Instead, if we are thinking of the future of Europe with an eye on the past, I would suggest the ancient and modern city of Brussels and, in particular, the very centre of that city, the heart of Europe's past and of Europe's future, the square called in Flemish the Grote Markt and in French La Grand-Place (the Great Square). I am always struck by the perfect proportions of that *place* or square. I can think of only one other square with comparably neat proportions and similarly venerable connections with a great historic past and with as much seductive architecture, and that is the Piazza San Marco in Venice, which stands quite fittingly at the other extremity of Europe.

The Grote Markt or Grand-Place in Brussels is for me a perfect image in stone of our European political culture at its finest: a balance, and accommodation, of the various seats of power. Next time you visit the square, stand in the middle and you will see on one side the Palace of the Dukes of Burgundy, the seat of princely power. Opposite is the beautiful Town Hall with its superbly slender tower and its gabled roof spotted with dormer windows as in a canvas by Vermeer; this is the seat of municipal power, built in the fifteenth century when the dukes of Burgundy were at the pinnacle of their fame and influence. Thus both types of power, princely and municipal, face each other across that square, almost as though in dialogue with each other although from their respective ramparts and across an appreciable distance.

On the shorter sides of the Grand-Place and pushing their way alongside the great public buildings are the beautiful, narrow, wide-windowed, gable-roofed houses of the ancient Guilds, houses built by the rich traders of late medieval Brussels who first established the power and the fortune of the city. These houses are the very image of wealth, of well-being and of ease with their gilded façades and their carved and sculpted tops. They jostle closely together, as if they really wanted to be in the first row and did not want to lose an inch in the tug-of-war that went on between the City, the municipal power on the one side, and the Princes' power on the other side. The merchants really want to be there, an essential part of the show. They complete the square. They make it fit, and fitting. As one stands in the centre of the Grand-Place today, I do not think it too fanciful to see in that square an incarnation in stone of the democratic accommodation of competing interests that our European political culture has been striving to achieve over the course of many subsequent centuries of struggle.

There is a further quality of the Grand-Place that I find suggestive: the very light, slight slope of the square itself. If we pursue for a moment my analogy between the physicality of the square and the political culture it embodies, you might think that this obliquity should indicate a lack of stability. But I would prefer to argue that, on the contrary, you have in that gentle declivity the little extra touch of madness that makes stability perfect. It is the imperfections, the roughage, the accommodation of inconsistency and of the eccentric, of the grand and the petty, the precise and the asymmetrical that is the very touchstone of the mature political culture we have developed. People from Brussels and all over Europe, rich and poor, old and young, congregate on the Grand-Place on a summer's night, mixing easily together and with their historic surroundings. On some evenings when the façades are floodlit, amplified music bounces back and forth across the great buildings so that the Grand-Place almost resembles an open-air ballroom. If you dance your way down the square to the bottom right-hand corner, you will reach the 'King of Spain'. Not the real one, of course. He was finally ousted from Brussels back in the seventeenth century. Today the 'King of Spain' is a great drinking house. On any of several floors of creaking wooden boards and tables and benches, looking out over the square through ancient lattice-windows, you can order any of a quite bewildering variety of slightly sour, rasping, pungent Belgian beers: the *'gueuzes lambic'*, the *'gueuzes kriek'*, the *'blanches'*, or the *'Cineys'*, or whatever takes your fancy. It is a real pleasure to drink those beers overlooking and overhearing the bubbling, babbling Babel of tongues below. It is almost as though one were in the midst of a Bruegel canvas, the very image of a multi-cultural Europe united in a common enthusiasm for diversity.

Now a sober thought surfaces. In the midst of that Bruegelian whirlwind, who would notice that all these palaces and ancient houses are not genuine? For none of these great buildings is the original erected there in Burgundian times. These are mock façades, copies of the originals, built not in the late Middle Ages but at the end of the seventeenth century and during the eighteenth, after the French Marshal de Villeroi had obliterated their predecessors on the orders of King Louis XIV during the wars of the League of Augsburg.

It has been quite common for the great democratic squares and *places* of northern Europe to be razed to the ground, flattened, pounded, bombed and shelled in the course of war, only to rise once more from their own ashes, and this has continued to happen during the flow of centuries to our own times. Take the city of Arras, for instance, in the north of France. If you drive along the motorway that links Calais with Paris, stop off if only to spend a few minutes on one of that city's magnificent pair of adjacent squares, a picturesque slice of the Netherlands set down in the north of France. Here too, as in the Grote Markt in Brussels, you can feel transported back to medieval times. Yet in Arras as in Brussels the historical setting is a copy, in this case reproduced after the First World War when the great squares were flattened by German and British artillery. Examples can easily be multiplied, particularly in the wake of the Second World War, as anyone who has visited Nuremberg or Munich or countless other German cities can easily testify.

An interesting question lurks behind all this replicated history. I have already suggested a link between imperfection and political maturity. I wonder whether there is not also a connection between true democracy, true freedom, and the impermanence of the models we revere. We do, after all, make a habit of adopting as symbols of our heritage objects whose original manifestation is no longer authentically available. The British 'Mother of Parliaments' is a pseudo-Gothic palace constructed in Victorian times, the French 'Assemblée' an imitation Greek Temple. I am not deriding the myths associated with these great artefacts. On the contrary, the belief that our modern democratic culture emerged gradually from profound historic roots is in itself one of the factors that helps nourish and perpetuate that culture. But we should recognise myths for what they are: stories and images and artefacts that may not carry the historic weight we popularly ascribe to them and which have more to say about the present and future than about the distant past. Just as democracy has continually to renew itself, so perhaps do the historical myths with which we sustain it. It is as though democracy can only thrive on the sharing – and then perhaps the shearing – of illusion, and can flourish only on the ruins of permanence.

An alarming thought? Maybe. And I am not advocating the death and destruction of our great urban centres or a preference for fake architecture. A genuinely democratic culture, however, like the carefully balanced life of an individual human being, is a fragile thing, the more valuable for the built-in impermanence of everything it embodies. The French writer, critic and poet Paul Valéry had this to say in the aftermath of the First World War: 'Nous autres civilisations, nous savons maintenant que nous sommes mortelles.' ('We civilisations know now that we are mortal.') This may sound like a bit of pompous French rhetoric, but it does contain an important truth, and one that was by no means self-evident until that period. For what we can now see as contributing to the strength and resilience of many of our great European cities is that they have had to integrate into themselves the notion of death and destruction which is always potentially lurking there, but at the same time they have triumphed over death and over destruction to become the great metropolitan centres that so many of them are today.

The historic transformation of Brussels contains further lessons. What business, for instance, did Louis XIV's generals have there in 1695? Why did Louis XIV not remain within the limits of his existing frontiers? Well, he was waging war, as he did almost throughout his long reign, fighting the rest of Europe in order to try to expand French frontiers far into the core of the rest of Europe and setting the pace and the pattern for those kings and dictators that were to follow him. I would even go so far as to say that there could have been no Hitler, and certainly no Napoleon, if there had not first been Louis XIV. Like them he was a little man with a constant need for self-assertion, an aggressive nationalist who played out his bellicosity on an international stage, hoping to adorn his own capital with the fruits of foreign conquest. Am I too harsh on the *Roi Soleil*? The French learn of the flowering of literature and the arts that occurred during his reign, and his grandiose palace at Versailles is one of the miracles of imaginative human construction, a symbol of power comparable to the Pyramids. But nowhere in the great regal city of Paris, or in its historic suburbs like Versailles or Fontainebleau, will you find a *place* as comfortable, as easy to occupy as the Grote Markt in Brussels. Most of our French squares are devoted to abstractions of power rather than to concrete notions, to concrete things. They are allegorical places, the Place de la Concorde, for instance, the Place de la Nation, the Place de la République, or indeed the Place de la Bastille (once very concrete and something which had to be pulled down, but of course an abstract symbol ever since).

Paris is a regal city, a royal city, dressed in Republican garb. Even the Place de la Concorde, *the* square in Paris, has nothing genuinely popular or democratic about it. Nowadays, it is for cars, not people. Historically it was devised in the eighteenth century by Louis XV, and at first named after him, as a sort of extension to the Tuileries, at that time the royal seat of power. By the time of the French Revolution (after which it was renamed), it formed the stage on which both the king, Louis XVI, and a year later the radical populist Robespierre were beheaded. Thus both the monarch and the revolutionary were treated to the same show on that show square, or show-place, of Paris. After the Revolution the square was clearly in need of yet another name to obliterate the memory of the gory events that had taken place there; only then was it christened – of all things – 'Concorde'.

The French are very good at renaming places and creating the illusion that the places themselves are thereby changed. Mind you, renaming that particular square was evidently not enough. In the 1830s, another king, the gentle and rather ineffective Louis-Philippe, added something else: an obelisk brought up the Seine all the way from Egypt. With great difficulty this priceless ancient monument was raised on the Place de la Concorde and there it stands to this day, an exotic, oriental talisman erected in a square with a meaningless, abstract name as though to exorcise by magic the bloody chapter in French history that once occurred there.

Perhaps the closest Paris ever came to having a real 'popular' square, Brussels style, was in 1790. On 14 July 1790, on the very first anniversary of the storming of the Bastille, the French came together to celebrate a Festival they called the *Fête de la Fédération* – Federation Day or Federation Festival. They selected the largest of all the *places* in Paris, the Champ de Mars or the Field of Mars. Appropriately, this was originally the drilling ground for the Military School, the École Militaire that still stands at the southern extremity of this vast square. The *Fête de la Fédération* was a strange event. People turned up from all over Paris and beyond with spades and wheelbarrows and dug up the earth in the centre in an effort to make the square resemble a Roman stadium: the French Revolution was very strong on Roman symbolism, and this was after all the *Campus Martius*. The latter-day Diggers were determined to enjoy themselves.

Crowds poured into the Champ de Mars in huge numbers. The king was present. He had no choice; he had to be there and did his best to look pleased. The queen was there too. But she was clearly not amused, perhaps because she had to carry the *cocarde*, the tricolour badge, on her coif. Also present was the Marquis de Lafayette, who had recently distinguished himself in the American Revolution. His job was to marshal the recently created National Guard. The whole show had a look of order, a military look, about it.

Why were they all gathered there? What were they all supposed to be celebrating? Above all, of course, the first anniversary of the Storming of the Bastille. But they were also celebrating the altogether novel idea of France as a decentralised federation. Remember that the Assemblée Constituante made up of the three Orders had gathered to draw up a new Constitution and was making a lot of noise about the idea of political decentralisation, while the new *départements* were intended to have no representative of central government supervising their affairs. All this was unprecedented in France. At no stage in its history had it reached for such a degree of untrammelled political freedom. The Fête de la Fédération must therefore have been a brief moment of almost intoxicating optimism. What the people had struggled for was within reach at last, and perfect political fulfilment within sight. This was the true celebration, and for this they raised there, right in the midst of the Champ de Mars, an altar on which Mass was celebrated and oaths solemnly sworn. The Mass was led by Bishop Talleyrand, surrounded by 300 priests who all wore the tricolour scarf around their waists. And the oath to the idea of, in effect, a federated, decentralised France was taken by everyone including the king himself. For a moment, all were united in hope: religion, monarchy and the people.

It was not to last. The Fête de la Fédération and the optimism it engendered were washed away by relentless rain which turned the Roman stadium into a quagmire. By evening, most people were deeply dispirited. The queen must have looked particularly miserable with her wet tricolour *cocarde* on her cap. Decentralisation, federation: democracy itself got stuck in the mud that day, and the Revolution took an utterly different turn, raging on until the king and queen were beheaded.

History might have found fit to stop on that day and turn the Champ de Mars into a square similar to the Grote Markt in Brussels where all the emblems of power and politics could have been reconciled. But this was not to be. Today the Champ de Mars is simply a *jardin à la française*, a long neat quadrangle of dust and grass, a place for tourists, especially Anglo-Saxon tourists, who turn their backs on the École Militaire and stare upwards instead at our great Parisian *Dame de Fer*, the original 'Iron Lady', the 'Tour Eiffel' who took her place at the head of the Champ de Mars at the half-way point between the Fête de la Fédération and our own day.

I wonder if the British would have let the rain arrest their progress towards popular democracy. It is worth remembering that the great climactic Chartist rally in London in 1848 was also washed away in a downpour, and this perhaps played its part in ensuring that Britain would have no revolution in a year that saw the overthrow of so many Old Regimes in Europe, including that of poor Louis-Philippe. But we French tend to think that the British behave much more stoically under rain, that they have learned over the centuries to cope with it. And in any case I suspect British rain helps the parks and squares to become more grassy.

This is not a trivial point. Consider for a moment the differences between, say, Hyde Park or Kensington Gardens and the Jardin du Luxembourg in Paris. British parks are large and green, built and cultivated with a deliberate eye to asymmetry, packed on sunny summer days with people sprawled informally in every imaginable posture. In France, the trees are calculatedly equidistant, all of a size, their roots as often as not carefully protected beneath a standard issue metal grille. Much of the surface between and around them is not of grass but of grit. And this difference can be repeated throughout the length and breadth of both countries. Where the British have gardens, the French have a town square named after a notable date or an elevated concept. Where the British have greens and commons, the French have landscaping. Where the British bring the countryside into the towns, the French bring urban planning into their rural estates. Compare the supreme calculation of the gardens of Versailles, for instance, with the subtle undulations of Blenheim.

There is something deliberately external, aggressive and assertive about the way the French mark the significance of things. Nothing in the recent American or Australian Bicentenary celebrations was quite so bold or brash as, for example, the building of the Glass Pyramid in the front courtyard of the Louvre. The great landmarks in the journey towards a democratic culture have been overt, external, explicit and remembered as such. All French children know how their forebears built barricades, destroyed buildings, stormed fortresses, took to the streets, rioted among the squares, palaces and *places* – and wrote it all up in noble prose. It was as though, being genuine idealists, the French could never find a space adequate to embody their values. The British, on the contrary, seem to have undergone a constant process of interiorisation, the gradual refinement of the game of 'indoor politics' practised by players who would be loath to write down the rules of the game but who pride themselves on being able to play it to perfection by ear, as it were. There is no equivalent of the Grote Markt in Paris because our squares are too grandiose, too abstract. The nearest equivalent in Britain is probably to be found not in Trafalgar Square or even Speakers' Corner on the edge of Hyde Park, but in that indoor haven of relaxed, classless, generous sociability: the pub.

Now that our British and French destinies are increasingly converging within a wider Europe, how are we to reconcile our two cultures? Of course, we share similar democratic values, but the paths that have led us there are very different. How will we accommodate a largely abstract, external, constitutional definition of democracy with a conception of democracy as a symphony to be played only by those who already have the music in their heads? It will not be easy. It is hardly likely that the French will ever take to cricket or even recognise the subtle shadings that differentiate a cricket pitch from a village green, a park or a lawn. Neither (I hope) will a family of Englishmen ever try to picnic in the midst of the Place de la Concorde.

Perhaps we can both learn from that great, sloping Grote Markt in Brussels, where one can walk and talk and sit and eat and drink and dance and listen to music and buy flowers, all the while surrounded by the visible reconciliation of historical conflict. This is the image

that squares best with my conception of the Europe of 1992 and
beyond. Here is a daily and nightly Fête de la Fédération, a tangible
yet informal linking of languages and cultures, a fluid, flowing
monument to a multicultural future bounded by the façades of an
apparently immutable past. If you require a monument (in the words
of Christopher Wren from his memorial in Saint Paul's Cathedral)
look around you.

2

In Pursuit of the Golden Fleece

With all the digging up of data that went on in connection with the Bicentenary of the French Revolution, and the earnest quest for new interpretations of its origins and significance, it was easy to lose a sense of perspective and to become a bit perplexed. That perplexity, however, is nothing new. People, even the sharpest minds, were often nonplussed at the time. Listen to that enigmatic but imaginative figure, the Marquis de Sade, who said in 1791:

> J'adore le roi, mais je déteste les anciens abus; j'aime une infinité d'articles de la Constitution, d'autres me révoltent. Je ne veux point d'Assemblée Nationale, mais deux Chambres, comme en Angleterre ... Que suis-je à present? Aristocrate, ou démocrate? Vous me le direz, s'il vous plaît. Car pour moi, je n'en sais rien.

> (I worship the King, yet I loathe the past excesses. I like a large number of the items in the new Constitution, while others revolt me. I do not want a National Assembly; I want two Houses, as they have in England. What am I at the moment? An aristocrat or a democrat? Please tell me. I myself cannot tell.)

De Sade was one of the very few prisoners left in the Bastille in the days before it was stormed by the people of Paris in the summer of 1789. He could hardly claim to have been an authentic democrat or revolutionary himself, and indeed the Revolution was to send him back to jail in 1793. Yet he was to play his part in the Revolution in Paris as a member of the section of 'Piques', redolent of those real revolutionaries, the 'sans culottes', walking barefoot in the streets of Paris, carrying a pike on top of which, in image if not always in fact, was the blood-drenched head of a French aristocrat. De Sade did not go in for this kind of grotesquerie, but he did help a lot of people fleeing arrest to reach England, and he also tried to stop some of the informing and false reporting that went on at the time. Indeed, this is why he was again arrested, jailed in 1793 and sentenced to death on 26 July 1794. In the event, luck was on his side in the form of the endless red tape with which the Revolution tied its own hands, and the Marquis de Sade was reprieved - just in time to see the guillotining of the greatest firebrand of them all, Robespierre, two days later on 28 July.

Now, you might expect that, being myself a northerner, and so far as I am aware no Sadean or Sadist, I would have a sneaking sympathy for Robespierre, the lawyer from Arras, a town we mentioned in the last essay and with which my own name suggests a historical family link. And indeed it is easy to admire a man who passed from the obscurity of dull, banal provincial life to the peaks of fame and glory: the very model, almost, of Stendhal's Julien Sorel. Personally, however, I have no love whatever for Robespierre, for he represents not the rise of France but its total downfall. Robespierre lived and died for a brand of almost religious nationalism: a quasi-mystical belief in the nation that led not to the triumph of the people of France but to the follies and defeats of Napoleon.

The reasons why Robespierre and his ilk shot to prominence at the time of the French Revolution lie deeply enmeshed in centuries of previous history. Clues lie everywhere, even in such apparent trivia as his name: his first name was Maximilien. Maximilien de Robespierre hailed from the minor aristocracy and was named after the Emperor Maximilien I of Austria. This is the man who, by marrying Marie de Bourgogne, daughter of Charles the Bold of Burgundy, enabled the Duchy of Burgundy to survive defeat by the French King, Louis XI, and then to become an Austro-Spanish province. Much of the area that we now think of as the north of France and its Lowland neighbours spent four brilliant centuries first as the great Duchy of

Burgundy and then as part of the vast, cosmopolitan Habsburg Empire. Thus Arras, the town from which Robespierre came in the north of France and where I too have my roots, embodies a cultural legacy far richer than 'Maximilien' de Robespierre himself acknowledged.

Arras was a major city throughout much of the Middle Ages, one of the wealthiest cities in that part of Europe. The dukes of Burgundy held court there, an early form of parliament, as they did in such towns as Lille, Brussels, Tournai, Dijon and Bruges. That list gives some idea of the extent of the Duchy of Burgundy: it was about the size of present-day Holland and Belgium, overlapping with them on the map, though much of it a little further south and west. Burgundy was, in effect, a sovereign state, a buffer between the great monarchies of early France and England and between them and the northern outposts of Habsburg power to whom it was later annexed. A great city like Arras, therefore, stood literally at the crossroads of history. If you visit the city today and look at its magnificent twin squares surrounded by their great Amsterdam-like gabled houses, you will see the tangible legacy of an immense past fortune built on wool trading and 'Arras'-making (those famous tapestries or hangings which were used by all the courts of Europe, and through one of which, if you remember, Prince Hamlet kills Polonius).

In its great days, when the Duchy of Burgundy was part of the Emperor Maximilien's northernmost domains, the city of Arras was very much Flemish or Netherlandish in outlook and style, and it still retains this aspect today. The prosperity of the city was only finally arrested in the eighteenth century as young Maximilien de Robespierre was growing up, a process greatly accelerated by activities put in train by Robespierre himself.

When Robespierre was in his teens, there was still a hint of the great cultural centre the city of Arras had once been. As a young man he attended a literary society called the Rosati (which still exists today) because he had aspirations to become a poet. When only twenty-five he was elected to the Arras 'Académie', the local version of the Académie Française, started by Richelieu. Robespierre was elected deputy for the province of Artois to the États Généraux, the States General, where people at first derided the young man's eloquence and made fun of his accent just as they were to do of other youthful provincial leaders like Napoleon from Corsica, Hitler from Austria or Mao Zedong from Hunan. People from northern France, with their Burgundian and Austro-Spanish cultural roots, had long been regarded as foreigners by the rest of France. This made the young Robespierre more determined than ever to prove the authenticity of his Frenchness. In this he was a direct spiritual descendant of Louis XIV; you proved your commitment to France by destroying anything around you that did not qualify. When French troops took Arras from Spain in the mid-seventeenth century in an expansionist mood that under Louis XIV was eventually to engulf Brussels, they not only contributed mightily to the wholesale economic decline of the region but also helped generate the narrow, national conception of France and its frontiers which was to be endorsed a hundred years later by the French Revolution. Hence the endless and bloody quarrels between Germany and France that were to render the coming of a united Europe almost impossible for two further centuries.

This is the extent of my dislike for Robespierre, therefore. For he unwittingly – perhaps unconsciously – represented the petty French nationalism that flies in the face of the much bigger historical legacy of Arras and the old Duchy of Burgundy of which the city was once part. And it was this French nationalism that inhibited, really until our own times, a new reconciliation of the Latin and German cultures that flowed so creatively in the Arras of the Burgundian Dukes and the Austro-Spanish Emperors. And if the nationalism of Robespierre represented a betrayal of the legacy of Arras, an acceptance of the destructive patriotism of Louis XIV, its shrill cry continued to echo long after his own death as the 'Nation en Armes' pursued its doomed campaigns against first the English and later the Prussians.

It is unfashionable, I know, to interpret the past with the benefit of hindsight, and even more unfashionable to elevate the medieval past to a status far greater than, say, the eighteenth century Enlightenment as a model for the kind of society we are ourselves trying to erect. You may perhaps cast me as some quixotic knight in search of the Holy Grail, perhaps as a latter-day Jason in pursuit of an unfindable Golden Fleece or a Theseus trying to slay the Minotaur of European nationalism. As a matter of fact, the Golden Fleece is a peculiarly appropriate image as it was the symbol adopted to represent Burgundy at its height in the fifteenth century at the time of Philippe Le Bon, Duke Philip the Good. Why the Golden Fleece? Well, the immense wealth of Burgundy was based on wool, the trading of wool, and the making and trading of cloth. Think of that perfect picture, the *Adoration of the Lamb,* by the Van Eyck brothers that you can still see in the Cathedral of Saint Bavon in Ghent. The Lamb is there of course for its Christian symbolism. But it is placed in the centre of the canvas because it also epitomises the fortune of the country. Look at the lusciousness of the grass carpeted by a rich variety of local flowers. That mirrors the lusciousness and the gloss of the wool of the lamb, whose very blood flows beautifully with its rich red colour, as if it were some sort of Burgundian wine in the very process of transubstantiation. And in the foreground stand the Elect, pompous, grave, fully-fed, fully-fleshed, the very cornerstone of Burgundian success.

Burgundy, the forgotten kingdom, was no historical backwater. In the fifteenth century it had a flourishing culture able to rival the Italian cities of the Renaissance. A real Quattrocento of the North was taking place there, a cultural explosion of astonishing power and range: a polyglot, polymath, polyphonic and polycentric culture. Polyphony in music, indeed, can stand as a metaphor for Burgundian culture as a whole, an image of the aspiration towards the harmonic accommodation of conflicting interests that we nowadays call democracy. A polyphonic piece of music is the sound equivalent of that great central square in Brussels we discussed in the last chapter where the demands of the people and the aristocrats, of the dukes and kings and merchants, jostle each other for position across the reverberant stones of history. This is the essence of the great polyphonic work of Guillaume Dufay, Gilles Binchois, Jean de Ockeghem and Josquin des Prés: Burgundians all, yet men of European culture, influenced by France, Italy and Germany, composers whose genius fed back in its turn into the mainstream of European art, through the great Lutheran masses of Bach and into the symphonic structures of Romanticism.

If musical polyphony was one aesthetic counterpart to the development of democracy, another can be seen in the painting that flourished in Burgundy: the delicate miniatures of the German-born Memling, or the big bold works of the Van Eyck brothers. The Van Eycks had an irresistible way of bringing the images of the time across the centuries to us today. The subjects they chose were, as we have already seen, traditional enough: Jesus on the Cross, the Lamb of God, the Virgin Mary and so on. But just as the Lamb would also become a symbol of the wool on which Burgundian wealth was based, so they would drape the body of the Virgin, for example, in colourful Burgundian cloth, rich, soft and velvety rather as a fashion designer of our own times, a Christian Lacroix, will indulge his personal whim when dressing his clients. All ranks and stations of life appear there in the paintings of Burgundy. Women were there in their own right; not just as dubious emblems of national virginity or in military guise, like Joan of Arc, but also as themselves, as the mothers and daughters and sisters and lovers, the workers and the homemakers and the cooks. For remember that, in addition to painting and music, cooking was almost as revered an art. We are in the historical home of those rich, red Burgundy wines with deep poetic names such as Nuits St Georges or Vosne-Romanée, and the cooks at the court of Burgundy were highly trained in the subtle art of creating wine-based sauces. There is a word in French, *le liant*, which dictionaries translate as suppleness or pliability. The *liant* is the 'X' factor which makes that rich Burgundian sauce cohere, which literally 'links up' its various ingredients to make it flow so beautifully and smoothly.

This was a culture that looked for wider connections, that linked the apparently separate, that flowed freely beyond its own natural confines. You find *liant* – very literally – in the work of the Van Eyck brothers who were among the first to use linseed oil in painting, to make the painting flow more easily and to dry less fast. And the Burgundians had *liant* also in the field of diplomacy, in politics, where, for example, Duke Philip the Good for forty years managed to benefit Burgundian interests by integrating them with the see-saw rivalries of the French and the English.

If I had been born in Burgundian times, in 1439 instead of 1939, though at the same place near Crécy on the very borders of the French kingdom and the Duchy of Burgundy, I would have had a real choice of cultures available to me: Burgundian (or Flemish), English and French. Perhaps I would have followed the example of the chronicler and poet Jean Froissart, who was to write in French for the English court and whose *Chronicles* tell among other things of the epic Battle of Crécy in one of the most vivid and brilliant pieces of early descriptive journalism. The French would have labelled me a traitor for my pains, for Crécy was the scene of one of the great English victories. But of course that fate may still befall me. After all, the reason I have been dwelling on the history and culture of late medieval Burgundy is not, of course, as a mere academic or antiquarian exercise.

You will have understood, I am sure, that the Burgundy of Philip the Good, that obscure Duchy that few nowadays can place with confidence on a map and on which there are very few books, certainly in French, is for me a wonderful model of the kind of multi-cultural Europe that I feel we have once more within our grasp five-and-a-half centuries later. If we are to face the future with confidence, we must face the past with honesty. Burgundy was not a minor provincial outpost of France, or a mere step on the road to the eventual independence of Belgium in the 1830s. The Bruges or Brussels or Liège or Arras of the fifteenth century would have been a great cultural metropolis. And this is why I cannot help feeling frustrated when I see that marvellous city of Bruges being used as a platform from which to launch a crusade to retain the old nationalisms of Europe, as though we had not yet overcome, or moved beyond, the cataclysmic tragedies that European nationalism has produced. In Burgundian times, Bruges was the most cosmopolitan of centres, full of artists and artisans, merchants and bankers speaking various languages, some coming from Italy or down from Germany and all gathering there under the wise guidance of Duke Philip the Good. If Bruges was prosperous at the time, it was precisely because it was multi-lingual, because it was multi-cultural, because it patronised the arts and could spread its music and its painting, its wines and its wools, all over the known world.

So forgive me if I dote on that almost mythical land of Burgundy as an antidote to the sour grapes of Nationalism. As early as the thirteenth century there was founded in Arras one of the first Guilds of Poets, and these poets enjoyed the patronage of the Count of Artois and also that of some of the wealthier merchants of the City of Arras. They celebrated love, wrote fearfully of death, and elected annual princes of poets rather as the city elected its mayors. It is the poetry of these medieval Burgundian minstrels which forms the very cornerstone of the French, Flemish and English poetry of subsequent centuries. Its echoes ring down across the ages to the songs of Jacques Prévert or Jacques Brel.

One of my tasks – my pleasures – in recent years has been to try to reweave this thread, this *liant*, linking the vibrant cultural pluralism of medieval Burgundy to the re-emerging European culture of our own times; to help weave anew, perhaps, the Golden Fleece of Philip the Good while not losing sight of the complex warp and woof of subsequent history. This is a delicate matter, one for which neither Robespierres nor de Sades are called for. The aggressive nationalism of the populist lawyer, no less than the enlightened indecisiveness of the cynical aristocrat, has little place in the new Europe now emerging. I would rather tunnel further back for models of the future – *reculer pour mieux sauter* – and look to the Duchy of Burgundy for inspiration. The creators of the new, larger Burgundy require a touch of English humour, a sprinkling of French wit, a dose of Flemish truculence, and above all an imaginative and tolerant dedication to the polyphony of a genuinely democratic culture.

3

Bruegel's Babels

I was invited to talk on Belgian radio about my book *Le Génie du Nord* (Genius of the North), an extended essay on the north and 'northernness'. The interviewer, a young Francophone Belgian poet, asked me tongue-in-cheek if I was not nervous about sounding too *exotic* in my professed admiration for Brussels. Cheek in tongue I firmly said no.

In general, the French seem to have two categories of opinions about Belgium. Most see the Belgians as lower and grosser caricatures of themselves. 'Belgian jokes' portray the typical Belgian as naive to the point of stupidity, always taking things literally. The French poke fun at Belgians' slowness of speech and unsophisticated accent, rather as the English sometimes make fun of the Irish. The second category consists of the enthusiasts: people who embrace as supremely Belgian all that is best in Flemish art and architecture. Wrong on both counts! Since the Belgians themselves have a talent for self-derision, their predicament is quite hopeless, but I sometimes suspect that they rejoice in their hopelessness, that they make an art of it. Belgium is the home of the strip cartoon (remember Hergé?) and of a rollicking sense of humour that the French with their supposedly refined sensibilities could never have invented and often cannot appreciate.

My Walloon interlocutor was effectively placing me in the second category: that of well-educated Frenchmen who mistake Flanders for the whole of Belgium and who invariably tell French-speaking Belgians of the splendours of Bruges and Ghent, how Antwerp is a lively harbour and how they adore the Flemish school of painting. His implied accusation had point. For had I not emphasised the

Amsterdam-like quality of Brussels, had I not compared all those gables and dormer-windows to so many paintings by Vermeer? Worse, I had even gone on about the beauty of the scarlet tulip fields of Holland extending toward the sea and sky which I said had made me feel as though I were present at the creation of a masterpiece by Van Gogh.

What can be more of a cliché, my interviewer cracked, than a field of tulips! I too turned a glaring red as I counterattacked. How can you be so self-deprecating, so lacking in self-assurance, I asked, as to rail at my simple compliment to everlasting beauty? Clichés are only repeated because they contain important kernels of truth; the ineffable majesty of the Dutch tulip-fields suggests a time-worn image only to those who have never had a sense of colour in the first place! I calmed down. But I meant what I said. I exult in colour, am hungry for it and when I see it extending to infinity under the sky I gasp with admiration. And my admiration has been nourished by the magnificent canvases of the Flemish or Dutch schools in the great galleries: the Rijksmuseum in Amsterdam or the National Gallery in London.

The ambiguity of being a Belgian today, most of all a Walloon Belgian coming from the French-speaking area that extends east and south of Brussels towards France and Germany, lies in feeling twice negated: first, by the rapidly developing Flemish community to the west of the country, largely Catholic farmers with a higher birth-rate than the socialist factory workers in Wallonia; and second, by France itself which pays such scant attention to its little neighbour. A French-speaking Belgian intellectual — perhaps like my radio interviewer — will thus be inclined to look to Paris for recognition and to be especially diffident, even contemptuous, towards the rare French citizen who declares a love of Belgium. For the Belgian will assign that French man or woman to the second category: the shallow snobs who see all that is valuable in Belgium as being in effect Flemish. The Belgian will assess such a person as an outsider, wielding little influence in Paris, and therefore unlikely to be of any help.

National frontiers have a lot to answer for. They lie not only in space but, more insidiously, in the mind as well in that they induce tortuous ways of thinking. The very fact of Belgium's independence as a nation state since the 1830s, for example, may have made it not easier but harder to build up a genuine bilingual culture and to elevate this dream to the category of myth. Back in the High Middle Ages when the Burgundian dukes ruled the United Provinces, Charles the Bold is reputed to have had command of seven foreign tongues. It is hard to believe that so educated a prince could have been the nasty character that French historians made him out to be in the following centuries. But it was in French interests to denigrate Charles the Bold, for his defeat by Louis XI in 1477 was supposedly a victory for the nascent power of France. As a result, Francophone Burgundy was cut in two. The northern part went to the Austrian Habsburgs, the southern part to France. And that frontier is still there, taken for granted on either side, the northern Francophones closeted with their Flemish neighbours and cut off from the French by a national boundary. What cultural effects are produced by this kind of political division?

Some claim that a long-suppressed culture can produce totally original artefacts which a normal flow and development might not have produced. Thus the slower pace at which the French language evolved on the Belgian side, hampered as it was by the ponderous proximity of German and Flemish, is sometimes said to account for a bursting and flowering of a peculiarly Belgian form of 'nonsense' as in the poetry of Michaux or the jokes of Raymond Devos, or the visual jokes of painters like Magritte and Delvaux. Yet I am inclined to think that that surrealist imagination was already there in medieval times. There was, for instance, the poetry of *fatras* (nonsense poetry) produced by the school of Arras. And there was the painting.

As an adolescent, I remember my intense response to the world of Bruegel. His was an art of locality, of space. My northern sympathies have always been attracted to the famous picture of 'The Hunters in the Snow'. I love those men trudging home in the crunching snow, their backs bent under the weight of furs won the hard way. Each bears his whole fate on his back, as it were, not caring about the insouciant community of children and women enjoying the ice down in the valley but instead reflecting gravely on the experiences of the day. Then there is that strange mountain range in the background which contrasts oddly with the foreground of moderate northern hills and slopes. They seem to represent the limits of the known world; a token too, if you like, of the Renaissance that lies in wait, about to disrupt the age-old stability of that precarious peasant community. But of course they are also the true Alps that stand station on the Habsburg route from Brussels down through Central Europe, sealing off France in the process from the wider European culture. It was to seal itself off further in later centuries. In a way I would be ready to agree with my Belgian interviewer when he accused me of exoticism. From the eighteenth century onwards, French culture has been literally 'exotic'; guilty of an inner exoticism, retreating from the rest of Europe to *cultiver son jardin*.

For me, rediscovering the north has nothing to do with some romantic Ossianic revival. I may have an idealised vision of Belgium or the Netherlands, but they were home to a genuine pan-European culture, mixing north and south, east and west in their very constitution. France, by contrast, gradually shut itself off from its neighbours because they were mainly Protestant, enjoyed freedom of the press and freedom of thought, and in short were regarded – and resented – as democracies ahead of their time. After Burgundy was divided and much of it passed to the House of Habsburg, French attention moved even more decisively away; the new centre of gravity was the South, Italy, the Loire Valley. The poet Lemaire de Belges, a mercenary, wrote the *Concorde des Deux Langages*, French and Italian, and our link with 'latinity' was further established by the Medici, the Concini, the Mazzini and the Buonaparte. The very year my book *Le Génie du Nord* was published and entered for the Medici(!) Prize, the prize was eventually awarded to an Italian critic for a book about the *Ruins of Rome*.

I love Rome and I love the South and do not wish to deprecate the now traditional French interest in the culture of the Mediterranean. But when that interest excludes others it can impoverish rather than enrich, and I have no doubt that our French sensibilities would be greatly enriched if we could re-establish our historic links with our neighbours to the north and east. This is not only desirable (for any cultural *rapprochement* must bring benefits); it is becoming critical. For the historically divided and even marginalised culture of Belgium is rapidly acquiring a central position as we fumble towards the implications of an increasingly united Europe.

Take the question of language. The linguistic rivalries that have dominated much of Belgian political life for the past fifty years contain lessons and warnings that might, writ large, be applicable to Europe as a whole in the decades to come. People ask, crudely: what language for Europe? To which everybody answers *in petto*: English. The British are delighted if a little embarrassed, the Danes and Dutch do not mind too much, and the French sulk in their tent. But can or should linguistic matters be planned and decreed or are they to be left to a free market competition? Questions such as these arise from the utter novelty of the task of building Europe as a nation. But why should one language be dominant? Are unilingualism or rivalry *à la Belge* the only models? Perhaps one might point in another direction, to Switzerland, a country of similar size to Belgium, having more languages foreign to each other, and yet enjoying comparative linguistic peace. However the Europe of the future takes shape, some accommodation will have to be made between the many linguistic and cultural traditions that jostle alongside each other, perhaps creating a new model more positive than that so far developed in any of today's European nation-states.

My own career reflects in miniature something of what could be the emerging European pattern. I began as a humanities student, acquiring a degree in Latin and Greek, then turned my back on them to specialise in English. I started late. Twenty is not the best age to graft a foreign language onto one's tongue. It was painful but I did it, and I have now taught English literature for over twenty years at university level with immense pleasure. Yet I must confess that now and then I have qualms and feel something of an impostor, not having the legitimacy of a native speaker. Worse, I also feel something of a traitor to my own language, as though I had abandoned it to live with another. That is not true, of course. I live and work in France and French, write my books and poetry in French, and through my translations bring English language poets and writers to my own countrymen. Indeed, one reason I decided to specialise in English and not French was that, knowing I wanted to become a writer, I deliberately avoided having to study or analyse or explain to others the language in which I knew I wished later to express myself most freely. None of this, however, prevents me from experiencing occasional twinges of guilt and of insecurity as I continue to profess English to my students. A psychiatrist would probably diagnose that my personality was unconsciously in need of that uncertainty, of a mental life constantly at the frontier's edge. A professional linguist would doubtless demonstrate that my multi-lingual *persona* rests upon a fragile base and that *real* professors of English should learn their language much earlier.

Perhaps. But if my inner doubts have personal explanations they may also suggest wider lessons. For I find myself a kind of pan-European guinea-pig learning late, but reasonably successfully, how to operate in a languange and culture not originally my own. My linguistic lack of assurance, certainly, is archetypally French. Indeed, the French have been worried about their ability to speak other people's languages – and even to speak their own properly – ever since France was constituted as a nation. There must have been a sense of original weakness, or original sin, for a strong man like Richelieu to have felt the need to create the Académie Française, an elite mechanism designed to protect and purify the French language. No other European nation has so arbitrarily made language a political issue as the French have done from the sixteenth century onwards. What did they fear? Was there already a threat from English? Not in the least! France at that time was by far the more populated country of the two. Latin had been dropped as the lawyers' tongue for more than a century and French was well on the way to becoming the international language – *lingua franca* – of diplomacy and high society. No; Richelieu's attempt to dig a linguistic moat around France reflects a much deeper insecurity, or cultural xenophobia perhaps, that was later to take more aggressive ideological and military forms and which probably lies at the root of my own restless determination to help create a bridge between French culture and the wider world.

Let me be even-handed about this. I would not want to ascribe cultural insularity to the French alone. The English may not have cramped their linguistic development with an 'Académie Anglaise' and the vastly greater richness of the English language is there for all to see and hear (and for foreign admirers to struggle with!). But English cultural xenophobia is notorious. Why did the English at Kilkenny enforce true apartheid, forbidding English squires to marry Irish girls or speak Gaelic? Why to this day are the British among the worst linguists in Europe? I wish they would teach their children to savour the French language as much as they have learned to enjoy good French food. Personally, I love speaking and reading and writing English, and the sense of cultural mobility I obtain – almost like the ecstasy of a plane taking off – when I am functioning well in a foreign tongue. My son speaks German and my daughter Spanish. None of us has much Italian, but I enjoy picking up whatever I can from the rapid-fire, pizzicato announcements delivered by the ravishing brunettes who act as 'Speakerines' on Italian television which we watch in Paris, courtesy of the miracle of cable and the millions of Mr Berlusconi. Of course, when we speak other people's languages we commit errors and distortions, but these can provide endless amusement, and corruption can sometimes be a source of creative progress. Where would the English be without *faux pas, fin de siècle* and the contents of most restaurant menus? Or the French if bereft of their imported English sporting terminology? Mind you, it is not just the British and the French who tend to be linguistic xenophobes: consider the militant linguistic nationalism that surfaces from time to time in French Canada, not to mention the two communities in Belgium. Or try talking German in Geneva or French in Zurich!

I come back to Belgium, to Burgundy, to Bruegel. One of Bruegel's favourite motifs was the Tower of Babel, which he represents in the form of a huge spiral-shaped lighthouse. This tallies with the multilingual talent of Charles the Bold at the Burgundian court. Again I am attracted to Burgundy to the point of cliché. A society is surely best assessed by the universality of the culture it creates. The Duchy of Burgundy, which nurtured the Van Eycks and Memling, Dufay, Ockeghem and Josquin, Bosch and Bruegel, is a culture to be envied, once a reality and still a model: a polyphonic community of free people coexisting in many tongues.

4

Highways of Freedom

There is no passport as effective as linguistic ability, no better way to enter the life and culture of others than to speak their language. But I discovered when still very young that an open-minded desire for cultural mobility might not amount to much unless you were also free to travel not just mentally but physically as well.

I was born on the eve of the Second World War in the village of Bernay on the edge of the Forest of Crécy in northern France, not far from the Channel. When my father, who had been made a prisoner by the Germans and worked in a labour camp down in Silesia, was released and sent back home, my parents decided to move further inland. So I left the sea and the forest and I missed them both very much. I had to adjust to a new geography, a landscape of plateaus and open fields, running away infinitely to the sky with here and there the spire of a church. That adjustment took time. I remember that two things in particular sustained my spirits. First there was my new village school. Normally French provincial schools were housed in a standard Third Republic brick building, but the school in this village had been destroyed by Allied bombing, utterly demolished. There was no building left to house a school again except for a magnificent disused country Château, protected by tall lime and linden trees. So the school was moved into that magnificent building, and this is where I spent much of my childhood and where I acquired the aristocratic dreams and Republican learning that led me to poetry.

The second thing that meant so much to me in those days was the main highway that went past the gates of the Château. It was the main road from the Channel ports to Paris. Sometimes, having nothing to do on a Sunday afternoon and getting bored, I would come to the edge of the highway just to watch the cars roll by. The cars that sent me dreaming most were those which carried a GB plate, the old Morrises and Austins. These cars were exotic because they carried whole families venturing over from a foreign land. Sometimes these families would stop by the roadside, open flasks of tea and eat little V-shaped – V for victory, I presumed – white bread sandwiches, whilst speaking an incomprehensible tongue. Those foreigners had prestige. They had prestige because they had movement. In my eyes they were the new aristocrats, because they had the right of passage, the right of way.

In a sense those British tourists were the mid-twentieth-century equivalents of those privileged travellers of the eighteenth and nineteenth centuries who went on the Grand Tour. What was once an upper-class preserve was now, before my youthful eyes, becoming democratised. I watched these newly motorised people with the privilege of mobility and I wanted to join them.

Freedom is never genuine without the right and the opportunity to move about freely. Countries that prevent or restrict their citizens from moving in and out cannot be said to be truly free. I was already developing this notion of freedom as a child, watching by the side of the road, dreaming all the time of extending my personal freedom. If they could come to France so easily, when would I be able to go to Britain? Little did I think in those days forty-odd years ago that I would live to see the eventual digging of a tunnel beneath the Channel to link France and England; a massive extension of that principle of freedom on which Europe was built and which, in time, should help end centuries of misunderstanding and hostility between the two countries.

The idea of a Channel tunnel dates back at least as far as 1802 during a brief respite brought about by the Treaty of Amiens in the chronic war between Britain and France. That tunnel was proposed by a French engineer called Albert Matthieu. He did not get far. One can easily imagine Napoleon's reaction (or Pitt's!) to such a project. But the idea tunnelled on and fifty years later, at the climax of British industrial glory, the great engineers of the day argued the benefits of laying a tube of steel on the bottom of the Channel. Queen Victoria herself approved of the idea, apparently advised to do so by Prince Albert. But Lord Palmerston remonstrated with the Prince and said bluntly: 'You would be of a different mind if you had been born on this island!' At this, the project was (as it were) grounded.

Now, another 140 years on, the Channel Tunnel idea is irreversible. Interestingly, the French seem to have been more consistently in favour of the Tunnel in recent years than the British. Perhaps the British are suspicious of that very enthusiasm. I have to say that the French are just as insular, mentally, as the British. Indeed, some French people regard the Tunnel as a greater threat to French identity than it will ever be to the British. For example, the English language, already universal, will be ringing in French ears more than ever from 1993 onwards, while French will probably continue to decline as an international language. Yet the great debate in France concerning the Tunnel has not for the most part been on matters of principle. The idea of a great technological link between our two countries has long been accepted in France and I think the French are psychologically prepared now for a closer physical union with Britain. Rather, the debate in France has been on the impact the Tunnel will have on the wider space we inhabit, the space of France, as well as that of the rest of Western Europe. People are asking what facilities, what benefits are going to derive from the opening of that tunnel? What are the wider opportunities it might help create?

Thus, ironically enough, on the British side − especially in the south-eastern part of England − many have been sceptical about the Tunnel and concentrated on the disruptions it might cause and the economic and ecological risks it might present. The Tunnel project has divided people. In France, on the contrary, cities − whole areas − have pulled together to try to ensure that the new Tunnel-related motorways and railway links will go through them and link them to what they see as a vast new hinterland. For the French, particularly up and down the whole eastern portion of the country, being left out is widely seen as tantamount to economic suicide.

However, it is not just a question of economics. For some time now, the French have been questioning some of axiomatic truths on which their nation has seemed to be established. Who are we? How French' is France? Is our historic identity not being diluted bit by bit

as we merge our destiny with that of our European neighbours? What
meaning remains to our historic frontiers, the famous 'Hexagon', in an
age of jet planes, satellite television, fax machines, nuclear bombs and
cross-Channel Tunnels?

One response to questions such as these has been to hide behind
the voluminous skirts of the past, the path taken by the somewhat
rigid, backward-looking, racist nationalism of Jean-Marie Le Pen and
his followers in the *Front National* (National Front party). With their
avowed desire to turn back the clock of history to a legendary time of
French whiteness and greatness, symbolised by their sentimental
near-idolatry of the mythic figure of Joan of Arc, the *Front National*
represents one reaction to the changes that beset modern France. It is
an extreme response, but no more so than the rootless 'here and now'
culture of some young people who are so captivated by the latest
waves that they have no awareness of the tides and the ocean. But
you can no more ignore the past than you can take shelter in it. The
political and geographical certainties of an earlier age may be eroding;
in which case, the only question is how best to shape the
configuration of the future.

Take, for example, that quintessentially French question of
'l'espace'; the nature of the overall space and the spatial subdivisions
we inhabit. If the Hexagon itself is secure, can the same be said of all
the rationalist principles of the French Revolution by which it is
carved up? The little cells of land called *départements*, for example,
each with a central town called a *chef-lieu* that could be reached within
a single day from its outer limits by anybody, peasant or bourgeois or
nobleman, riding a horse. These clear spatial images are already
becoming blurred, or at least less useful, with the onset of new rapid
means of communication, and this process will merely be further
emphasised by the opening of the Tunnel. What is being eroded,
therefore, is nothing less than the imposition of an eighteenth-century
Enlightenment rationality upon the spaces we inhabit. It is hardly
surprising that many find these changes threatening and fear that the
Tunnel will lead us deep into uncharted waters.

They need have no fear. For what these new developments point
towards is in many ways a revival of a much earlier period
pre-Enlightenment, pre-Renaissance medieval Europe when the

reference points by which people lived were on the one hand the local city or cluster of communities and, on the other, a trading and cultural hinterland that stretched far beyond what we now think of as the nation state. Space, then as now, was both immediate and transcendent, and the opening of the Tunnel is likely to increase both tendencies (at least as seen from France).

The question being asked by the opening of the Tunnel, therefore, is not so much which country is going to benefit from it; evidently both countries stand to benefit in various ways. But which city or region of northern and eastern France, which city of south-east England or even the English Midlands, will benefit most? Some claim the magical southern triangle of Montpellier, Barcelona and Toulouse in the south will profit most, which would be a sad irony for people living in northern France and south-east England. Others wonder whether, for example, Strasbourg will be weakened by the existence of the Tunnel in its rivalry against Brussels for the location of the ultimate capital of Europe. Then again, how long will Lille in northern France remain at the crux of the network for the TGV, our bullet trains? Will the by-passed harbours of Boulogne, Calais and Dunkerque be forced to team up in order to survive the competition from Rotterdam or Antwerp?

Questions such as these require answers that go far beyond the tidy spatial conceptions of the Enlightenment or the supposedly rational political sub-divisions of nineteenth-century nationalism. But in addition to the revival of the importance of the City – a reversion to medievalism in a way – there is a further pattern or model of space that is emerging, an American pattern. Just as some three or four hundred miles separate, say, Houston from New Orleans or Los Angeles from San Francisco and the Bay Area, so this is the kind of distance that lies between Amsterdam and Frankfurt, or between Barcelona and Lyon (or Milan). These are all new mega-centres, strategically distanced from one another in accordance with modern requirements, and they communicate directly with each other across national boundaries.

Personally, I am exhilarated by this mobility of people and goods and ideas between the great new urban centres of Europe. Mobility unfettered by national bureaucracies is, as I said at the outset, an

essential democratic freedom. How could I think otherwise? I who, as
a child in occupied France with my father in a labour camp in Silesia,
listened surreptitiously and illegally with my mother to the thrilling
sound of Winston Churchill's vigorous speeches and De Gaulle's *La
Voix de la France* (the Voice of France) crackling to us across the
Channel. Freedom, in my mind, was something available not far away,
a dangerous game, hard to reach or to receive, but all the more
exciting for that.

Our little village of Bernay lies between Montreuil and Abbeville
at the bottom of a sharp valley through which flows the little river
Maye. There, as a child, I used to visit a huge farmhouse of white
stone, where my mother bought eggs and butter and which had
formerly been an inn. You can still see it today, with its white gables,
its ivy-woven façade, its large yard and its stables waiting vacantly
for the now-dead sound of horses' hooves. When I was a youngster
the horse still helped plough and harvest the field, and provided for
me a direct link with past centuries when stage-coaches plied that
route between Calais and Paris. When my grandparents were born,
stage-coaches would have changed horses every twenty-four
kilometres at special inns. The inn at Bernay was one such: a
famous stage in its time on the road to Paris. Among its distinguished
guests and customers it could number Laurence Sterne, Tobias
Smollett and Victor Hugo and, some said, the Emperor Napoleon
himself.

Sterne in *The Sentimental Journey* and Smollett in *Peregrine Pickle*
have amusing part-autobiographical episodes clearly set in Bernay, as
I was to discover many years later when I came to read their books.
Famous writers such as these, and other Grand Tourists, would stop
there overnight *en route* to Paris, and thence to the south, perhaps to
Italy; they would flirt with the pretty chambermaids at the inn,
chasing them around the passages and corridors, and go on their way
the next morning. These men were to my mind nomads of liberty,
sowing their wild oats as they moved easily between one European
culture and the next.

I must have breathed in some of that air when as a child I visited
that inn by the side of the road in the midst of the war. Certainly I
grew up hating the restrictions of war and loving the idea of

circulation, irrespective of frontiers and barriers. I still do. But we have a long way to go, and our ambitions are pitifully limited. I was reading of the admirable Erasmus programme drafted for European universities and student exchanges. Its stated aim is to achieve the mobility of 10 per cent of all European students by 1993. Only 10 per cent! Six hundred years ago, in the High Middle Ages, students and teachers would pass in a regular flow from the Sorbonne to Florence, to Montpellier, to Oxford, then down to Padua and back. Compared to those medieval pilgrims passing from one sanctuary of learning to another, we are but mere cripples, tourists who culturally never really leave home, stay-at-homes of the mind.

I want to write my personal *Song of the Open Road*, different from Whitman's in that mine is a re-learning of the alphabet of the past. Which is why I think that tunnelling our way from both sides of the Channel will help achieve a mutual transfusion of history that should render British and French alike immune at last to our ancient, atavistic fears of each other: on the British side, a fear of the loss of insularity dating back at least to the time of Shakespeare and Elizabeth I; and on the French side, the fear of the invasion of our culture by the omnipresent English language. In my Open Road , these nationalistic fears have no place. Indeed Nationalism itself will be a thing of the past.

5

Travelling Back

Among British travellers making contact again with the Continent after the long interval of the Napoleonic Wars, John Ruskin was perhaps the most influential. His social thinking combined with his aestheticism has no equivalent on the French side of the Channel. But Ruskin's influence has waned somewhat. Like Matthew Arnold, he shares our modern preoccupations but brings to them utterly different solutions. Ruskin was a Romantic medievalist who followed a route pioneered by such eighteenth-century travellers of the mind as Thomas Gray and Horace Walpole who roamed in search of precious Gothic material in order to turn Strawberry Hill into a Castle of Otranto. Romantic medievalism is out of fashion in our materialistic times but Ruskin may still be able to teach us a lesson or two.

I first encountered John Ruskin through a selection of his writings edited by Sir Kenneth Clark, and I discovered to my delight that Ruskin had written a number of essays on medieval Picardy in Northern France. One is a description of the city of Abbeville, where I spent part of my childhood and had my family. Ruskin, travelling by stage-coach, imagines himself confronting the slope that still today leads motorists to the town centre, as if he had been some pilgrim of the past, some merchant plying his trade from fair to fair. Shedding his Victorian garb, he then proceeds to the moat, crosses a drawbridge and jostles his way into the maze of narrow lanes and gabled houses that nestle together roof by roof.

Ruskin did not have to stretch his imagination very far to obtain that vision. From what my parents told me, Abbeville before the Second World War retained much of its original aspect. The city walls had gone, but water still flowed along or across the streets, and into the river Somme by the banks of which flower-markets and cattle-fairs were held almost every day of the week. All this was only brought to an end by the incendiary bombs dropped by German planes in May 1940. One of their targets was the sugar-plant at the foot of the hill. Molasses freed by the bombs treacled its way down the gutters and across the roadway, turning the slope into a sweet, slippery nightmare for all the refugees who, fleeing from German troops, got stuck in an atrocious Lewis Carroll-like glutinous quagmire.

I was five when I came to the city for the first time just after the war was over. During the war, I had been protected from the shock of conflict by the thick screen of the Forest of Crécy. Our little village seemed scarcely touched by war. But when I was brought to Abbeville I could scarcely believe my eyes. Everywhere was rubble, razed houses and cellars gaping open to the sky. Everywhere, too, was water, not only rain water but water springing up from the spongy, marshy site on which Abbeville had been built from prehistoric times. Ruskin, in his various Victorian dissertations on the Somme valley, compares the nearby town of Amiens to Venice. How charming and flattering. My first memories of Amiens are of ourselves as gondoliers picking our filthy way through the potholes of a pathetically flooded main street.

This is where we, who have undergone the unspeakable horrors of the Second World War, part company with the mild, medieval-inspired Ruskinian view of the world. All his musings and reflections on the advantages of an organic, corporate society where creators and operatives would be harmoniously linked together in communities working for the promotion of beauty amount to Utopias in which we can no longer believe. Ruskin, like Karl Marx or Proudhon or Fourier in his desire to create the society of the future, essentially retreated into a romantic past. We who live in the late twentieth century have witnessed for ourselves what some of those glorious revivifications of a romanticised past have achieved.

My next encounter with Ruskin came through a translation into French of his 'Bible of Amiens'. By then I had moved to the University of Amiens. Like Abbeville, parts of Amiens too had been razed to the ground in May 1940. I had seen pictures of the flattened

town with the Cathedral emerging as some miraculously spared mast
on a ship completely adrift. Ruskin in his time had had a love affair
with the city of Amiens, almost as though he had transferred the love
of a man for a woman on to the many statues that adorn the
Cathedral. His warmest attentions were paid to the Virgin carved on
the southern portal whom he compares in her jolliness to a country
servant girl. One senses him happy in her company. But before he
paid homage to her, he confesses, he first walked into a pastry-shop
on the main street to order some flaky pastry (a 'religieuse' (creamy
eclair), one is tempted to suggest?). Ruskin is evidently one of those
nineteenth-century English churchmen who wanted more sugar on
their 'wafer' and turned to Rome as being more palatable than York or
Canterbury.

If you really want to know about the Cathedral of Amiens, you
would be better advised to use Baedeker than Ruskin, though
Ruskin's partiality for the little 'Gilded Virgin' is charming and his
French translator is Marcel Proust, no less. The real value of Ruskin's
book, however, lies in the theory he develops about the historical
origins of Gothic art. Ruskin harks back to Merovingian Europe and
writes about the Franks, a tribe from the banks of the Weser in
northern Germany. The Franks, as Ruskin tells it, started their fourth-
century invasion along with a whole host of other 'Barbarians' all
busily displacing the Romans at the same period. The Frankish tribes,
it seems, split into two: those who settled in France and were
eventually received into the Christian church (like Clovis), and those
who poured into northern Italy at roughly the same time and started
to establish the city of Venice.

What Ruskin is saying is that what was termed derisively 'Gothic'
art and architecture should actually be called 'Frankish' art or *art
français*. An interesting point this, because modern French critics,
obsessed since the 1870s with the Germans, do not particularly like to
be reminded of their Frankish ancestors. The French were, in origin,
'Gauls' or 'Celts' and their aesthetic sensibilities essentially
Mediterranean. These were the favoured theories. For years it was
a truism of French architectural history, for example, that our great
cathedrals, the jewels around the crown of Paris, were essentially
home-grown, a product of our own French (and therefore southern-

oriented) creative impulses. For me it took a nineteenth century Englishman to point out, even though in a fanciful and oblique way, the real truth. And a particularly ironic truth it is that the *Français* should have been persuaded by nineteenth century propaganda that in confronting the Germans they were fighting against Barbarians, against Goths, when their own cultural tradition – and even their very name – is itself of German origin. How tactless of our art historians to christen our cathedral architecture *art gothique*, which to French ears contains elements of 'barbarian', 'German' and 'northern' art: all, in their way, terms of abuse. And how percipient of Ruskin to peer through our language and labels to the profound truth that the historic core of French art lay in the Frankish tribes of Germany.

The Amiens of today leaves one with little chance of understanding how Ruskin could ever have compared it to the splendours of Venice. In his day it is possible that the rills and mills could have reminded a visitor of medieval times when a city of wealthy dyers pulled together to build one of the highest naves in the world. But Venice? Perhaps Ruskin was influenced here not only by his own love of both places, which may have suggested a bogus similarity between the two, but also by the French predilection for Mediterranean models and comparisons. The French quest for pseudo-southern aesthetic roots has skewed much more than merely our aesthetic vocabulary: it is not only that artistic labels like Breton and Gothic have long been terms of abuse, but the French tend to think of their entire post-Celtic history as having had essentially Roman (and Christian) origins. Such a conception is not only a distortion of the facts but further evidence of French insularity. They tried to have it both ways. By rejecting Gothic art as northern, German and alien, they revealed a series of utterly unfounded prejudices. But they did much the same when expropriating as peculiarly French the great cathedrals of Rouen, Rheims, Amiens, Orléans and Chartres, which were all built, so the historians tell us, as bastions of 'Frenchness' against the irreligious barbarians of the north. Of course these great edifices are *art français*. But *français* was in origin Frankish.

France, Ruskin suggests, was built on a conjuring trick. Put plainly, it is the story of northern invaders getting slowly sucked into a Roman ambience, forsaking their Germanic tongue and eventually being made to renege on any northern connection. Roman Catholic centralism was at work here, with the imitative support of the French monarchy! Ruskin's medievalism may sometimes be far-fetched but in setting us right about our Germanic origins he preaches a lesson that even today falls uneasily on some French ears.

What of Ruskin's importance back home in England? The home of romantic medievalism in England was the Lake District, and in some ways it still is. One day I found myself in the almost unknown town of Sedbergh. My friend the poet Basil Bunting had just been buried in the Quaker churchyard, a few yards from the impetuously flowing Rawthey of his song. I had not realised until then how close Bunting's Briggflatts was to Wordsworth country. I drove to Grasmere, noticing how the landscape changed from the almost forbidding severity of the bare Cumbrian hills into more leafy if equally spectacular valleys. On the whole I found Hawkshead more impressive than either Dove Cottage or Rydal Mount. The proximity of the grammar school to the churchyard on top of a hillock, and the cobblestoned lanes of the village by the lake where the young orphan would whizz past on his skates on freezing days, are more evocative to me than the Dove museum or the grandiose wetness of Rydal Mount (no wonder the children caught pneumonia there).

I could see how Bunting, in his rugged, private way, was a latter-day kinsman of Coleridge and the Wordsworths. But I found it harder to make the link in my mind between the Lake Poets and John Ruskin with his obsessive medievalism and his love of the Alps and of French cathedral cities. Yet here in Coniston was Ruskin's house: a gloomy place, I thought, evocative of a deep loneliness. Admittedly, an early September drizzle was blurring the contours of the lake which I am prepared to believe is of stupendous beauty. Ruskin's house itself has been made into a museum in which I was happy to see drawings in his hand of (among other things) Abbeville Collegial Church. But the junk and mess devoted to him in Coniston struck me as a pathetic illustration of Victorian bric-a-brac gone obsolete and dusty. I felt as if I were in a funeral vault just deserted by its vampire.

The vision of Ruskin's treasure-haunt reverberated back upon my impression of the lake, and I reflected once more on both the nobility and the fustiness of his antiquarianism. Increasingly, I felt that the only true mind to have come unscathed down to us from that period may have been that of Joseph Turner, the painter. He alone caught the genius of the time and place, transported it through his admiration for the Alps as far as Venice, but finally managed to build upon these influences and take his art forwards towards abstraction, futurism and modernity. Wordsworth and Ruskin seemed to me to have been made possible – and necessary – by the great divide of the French Revolution ruthlessly turning against the past. But they, unlike Turner, had staunchly camped on the far side of life's great divide, cultivating their 'organicist' vision of Nature and Life in the midst of their trees and slopes and springs. Theirs had been almost an art of the fantastic, an art of ghostlike vision, haunted by England more than inhabiting it. Alert as Ruskin had been to modern technology (unlike Wordsworth who had contempt for the modern city), theirs has basically been an art of suffering glossed over by a desperate quest for symbolic beauty.

I do not wish to deprecate the work and the memory of Wordsworth or of Ruskin: Ruskin provided me with a profound insight into the mists of French history and Wordsworth is obviously a colossal figure to whom we will return in later chapters. As faithful witnesses to what had been cripplingly left out by the French Revolution, as true indicators of the wealth wasted by the French in the shaping of their successive insularities, as 'negative Europeans' if I may put it so (negative in the sense that they put a stop to any claim by the French Revolution to universalism), that group of English artists deserves careful study and consideration. They tell the story of a European heritage dramatically cut in two. But one of the effects of their reaction to the French Revolution and its aftermath was to lock England up in its own home-made brand of insularity, a state from which Britain subsequently found it so difficult to escape. How ironic that some of the great visionaries of post-Revolutionary Europe should have helped plant the seeds of nationalism that were later to flower into world war.

6

Re-Crossing the Somme

The configuration of that part of Northern France from where I come is rather deceptive. It is is an extended plain which runs north of Paris to the Maas Valley at Namur in Belgium, north across to Germany and which then vanishes in the polders of Holland. There is no natural reason why anything should ever have arrested the mobility and circulation of people dwelling on that great flat expanse. Indeed, artificial political frontiers on principles differing from those of plain geography were quite a late arrival in our part of the world.

It is hard to understand, too, why these immense, open fields should have been one of the areas on earth most defaced by war. Where there are no natural barriers people have raised them and fought over them. This has frequently been the fate of the little river Somme, which flows calmly in its narrow bed for a mere 90 miles from Saint-Quentin to the sea and yet which has witnessed centuries of military manoeuvring as well as some of the goriest set-piece massacres in history.

During the Hundred Years War the Somme was crossed and re-crossed countless times: by the French cavalry, or the English archers of Edward III or Henry V benefiting from local informers on the best fords. Froissart, the Flemish chronicler of English kings, has a vivid description of the engineers of the English Army traipsing along the winding banks of the Somme sounding the depth of the water here and there for a possibility of passage.

The most colourful episode of all is surely the meeting between the French and English monarchs at Picquigny in 1485, arranged by the cunning Louis XI in order to bring the Hundred Years War to an end.

That episode is told by another chronicler of northern origin, Commynes (named after a little Burgundian town now in Belgium). According to Commynes, Louis XI arranged for the meeting to take place half-way across the Somme on a bridge made of boats, having first set up a trellised partition through which he addressed King Edward IV of England, as if not wanting to catch the germs of his adversary. One can imagine the two kings walking across water to talk to each other through the trellis above the river: what a perfect image of the absurd artificiality to which nations resort in their anxiety to establish frontiers. Not that France or England were yet real nations in the modern sense: there were no real national frontiers at that time; towns situated in the war zone could veer daily from one side to the other. Then, over the centuries, frontiers gradually hardened and hostility grew apace.

The Somme became almost professionally associated with war. This is where the French kings built their fortresses, set up garrisons and recruited their infantry. This is where English, French and German troops met and performed their bloody rituals again and again as if locked into a permanent theatre of war. And the greatest military show of all, a mutual massacre of awesome scale, they performed – perhaps we should say committed – in the summer months of 1916: the Battle of the Somme.

This, at least, is its name in Britain. Ironically enough, the name 'Somme' means little to the French on whose territory the battle took place. For most French people the north begins at the gateways of Paris, and the 'Somme' is merely a river somewhere between Paris and the Channel. It is in England, not France, that 'the Somme' means a battle. This was very well illustrated when a few years ago we had students at the University of Picardy over on an exchange from the University of Sheffield. Ours had gone to Sheffield to study drama (we have few good drama departments on our campuses which may help to explain the paucity of good new drama in France these days). The Sheffield students, for their part, were visiting in order to study film and cinema. They wanted to make a video; I told them that the first place we would visit for the shooting of the film would be the Somme. Good, they exclaimed, we have just done the War Poets. This is perfect field work, they said: perfect battlefield work. I was sorry to disappoint them, but I had to say no. When the French talk of the Somme, they mean the river.

We French sometimes display a dangerous tendency to forget about the First World War. It is true that to French ears the word 'Verdun' conjures up something of the massive slaughter of the trenches rather as the 'Somme' does for the British. But whereas the Great War can still evoke in Britain a sense of tragic waste, of heroic loss, a glimpse of what might have been, in France that war is regarded – if at all – as a meaningless massacre, an absurdity in which two armies exterminated each other without gaining an inch of ground. If the French talk about war at all, it is to the humiliation of the Second World War rather than the carnage of the First that they tend to return.

There are many reasons why the Second World War casts a darker shadow than the First. Millions now alive were directly affected. The Second World War was fought over fundamental moral issues of good and evil, and the entire future of humanity has been radically touched by its two apocalyptic events: the mass murder of Jews and the dropping of the atomic bomb. For the first time in history what was at stake in a sort of world-wide Darwinian conflict was the moral and even physical survival not just of the fittest but of mankind *per se*: far more weighty matters even than those raised by the waters of the Somme.

However, the Second World War in no way solved or dissolved the problems raised by the First and, if it is possible to think our way back through Auschwitz and Hiroshima to Verdun and the Somme, it is to the issues of 1914–18 that I wish to return. For these, I believe, have just as great a relevance to the new Europe we are struggling to create. A controversial view, I know, particularly in France where the First World War remains a dangerously silent minefield for the incautious historian. But I am a man of the Somme, born and bred on the fields of battle and used to picking my way through the minefields of history.

The First World War was primarily a conflict concerning frontiers. It arose from – and helped to perpetuate – complex issues of nationalism, of national frontiers, of national self-determination and sovereignty, all of which lie at the heart of today's debate about the

Europe of tomorrow. The Second, by contrast, was about systems of ideas: fascism, communism, and the need of nations to work together to defeat evil. In both wars the fate of Europe was at stake.

We Europeans still stand astride the two sets of issues, in a no man's land, as it were, between the two conflicts. Consider for instance, the nagging question frequently raised by today's right-wing parties in the West, the ardent nationalists. Why, they ask, should we want to dilute ourselves in a federation of nations of Europe? Have not national identities and frontiers always been our greatest safeguard? Regional cultural differences cannot be contained or eradicated simply by constitutional fiat. And why try to erode these differences anyway? Is this not precisely what gives Europe its immense richness as a civilisation? And was it not to sustain preserve these national identities that all those boys di~~~~ ~~~~rs and Picardy? The men of Versailles, they argue in effec~, ~e wiser than the men of Brussels. Thus, when we talk of lifting economic barriers by the end of 1992, a whole flurry of issues arise which really boil down to one ideological question: should we be aiming eventually to supersede national frontiers in the name of an economic ideal, the European Community? That is, should the multi-national imperatives of the Second World War take precedence over the nationalisms that fuelled the First?

The question is even more intriguing if we extend the enquiry to embrace Eastern as well as Western Europe and here, too, the seeds of some of today's pivotal questions were sown during the First World War. The overthrow of the Tsars in 1917 and their eventual replacement by the Bolsheviks had the immediate effect of taking Russia out of the War. Russian nationalism, such as it was by then, was devalued and the very name of the country reconstituted by its new leaders as the 'Union of Soviet Socialist Republics', a title which makes no reference to nationality or geography. Before long, 'Russia' was ruled by a Georgian, Stalin, whose systematic denial of local nationalisms was carried out with a barbarism equalled only by Adolf Hitler: two men who emerged from outside the mainstream culture they came to dominate and who could not abide deviation from the centrist norms they themselves established. But whereas Hitler pursued his imperialist aims under the pretext of bringing together

Van Eyck: The Madonna with Chancellor Rolin (Louvre, Paris). *The Bridgeman Art Library*

3. Bruegel: The Wedding Dance (Holbourne Museum, Bath). *The Bridgeman Art Library*

4. Van Eyck: The Adoration of the Lamb (Ghent Polyptych, Ghent, Cathedral of St Bavon). *The Mansell Collection*

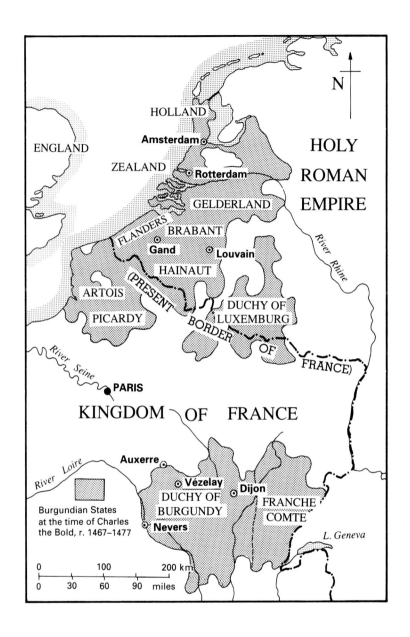

N

HOLLAND

Amsterdam

ENGLAND

ZEALAND   Rotterdam

HOLY
ROMAN
EMPIRE

GELDERLAND

FLANDERS

BRABANT

Gand

Louvain

HAINAUT

River Rhine

ARTOIS

(PRESENT

PICARDY

BORDER

DUCHY OF
LUXEMBURG

OF

FRANCE)

River Seine

PARIS

KINGDOM   OF   FRANCE

River Loire

Auxerre

Vézelay   Dijon

DUCHY OF
BURGUNDY

FRANCHE
COMTE

Burgundian States
at the time of Charles
the Bold, r. 1467–1477

Nevers

L. Geneva

0	100	200 km
0	30 60 90	miles

5.   Map of Burgundy in the Fifteenth Century. *Katrina Ellor*

6. Bruegel: The Tower of Babel (Kunsthistorisches Museum, Vienna). *The Mansell Collecti*

7. The Eiffel Tower under construction, 1889. *The Mansell Collection*

8. La Grand-Place (Grote Markt), Brussels. *Camera Press, London*

people authentically 'German' into a single large nation based on race, Stalin made no such claims. He may have used Russian nationalism as a temporary war-cry in 1941, but his attempts to 'Russify' the Muslims of central Asia or, later, the Latvians and Lithuanians around the Baltic were the very denial of nationalism. Both dictators despised and eliminated 'outsiders'; but Stalin did not have it in him to develop a countervailing system to bolster the spirits of those 'fortunate' enough to be within the magic circle.

At the beginning of the Second World War, the two dictators were in alliance. When it ended, Hitler's system of racially-based nationalism was defeated whilst Stalin's supranational communism was more firmly entrenched than ever. It now extended westward half way across Europe to the truce lines that were soon to be dubbed the 'Iron Curtain'. Throughout Europe, the Second World War left the idea of nationalism based on race lying in tatters and disrepute while everyone, from the Atlantic to the Urals, recognised the need for multi-national systems of mutual cooperation. In West and East alike a defensive alliance was developed, NATO and the Warsaw Pact, each dominated by its superpower patron. In Western Europe, local and national cultures continued to develop under a reasonably free rein; further East they continued to be severely constricted under Stalin and his successors.

History furnishes many examples of authentic cultures which have survived despite the most ruthless attempts at suppression; perhaps even because of them, for the attempt to stamp out a culture can give it a glamour, and those who sustain it a prestige, that might not have developed under more normal conditions. Thus it was with the Jewish *Conversos* (Jews forced to 'convert' to Christianity but who secretly maintained their faith) in post-Expulsion Spain; or, four-and-a-half centuries later, the Catalans who surreptitiously kept their language and culture alive under the dark decades of Franco. And thus it was in many parts of the Soviet empire where secret or *samizdat* newspapers would keep alive a flickering light of Armenian or Lithuanian or Uzbekhi cultural and ethnic identity. When eventually the lid was gently loosened by an enlightened new leadership in the Kremlin, the pot rapidly overflowed with a volatile brew of concentrated cultural nationalism. The brew was potent and was eagerly and rapidly

imbibed outside the Soviet Union by neighbours in Poland, Hungary
and elsewhere. No government intentionally decides upon the
erosion of its own authority, and nobody in the Kremlin advocated
the dismemberment of the Soviet Union or the Warsaw Pact.
However, the era of a uniform Soviet bloc is clearly over and the
greater leeway given to local and regional nationalisms seems here to
stay.

How do these tendencies look in the light of events further West?
Is there not a fundamental irony in developments on the two sides of
the old Iron Curtain? After all, the countries in the West are trying to
slough off some of the inhibiting barriers that lie between them just as
those in the East are rediscovering their national differences. If the
whole of Europe, and not just the West, is eventually to inhabit
Gorbachev's 'Common European Home', what kind of accommodation can be found for the fissiparous national cultures to which his
freeing of the reins has given such a fillip? Perhaps events in Eastern
Europe contain lessons for us in the West. Are we in Western Europe
in danger of losing part of our valuable and varied cultural heritage in
the process of easing the economic links between us? Perhaps genuine
freedom consists – as so many are asserting in Eastern Europe and as
we ourselves used to assert a century ago – in the proper
maintenance of nationhood based on a common culture. These
arguments have strong appeal to those on the political right in France,
Britain and elsewhere. Committed Europeans reply to this that they
want to create a larger nation out of states that for so long used to
war with each other. But then one may wonder if by doing so
Western nations are not unwittingly fusing together explosive
elements from both world wars: grafting the nationalism of 1914 and
Versailles on to the spirit of wartime cooperation that later flowered
in the form of NATO and the Marshall Plan.

We may have survived two world wars but we have not outlived
them. The two wars still war with each other in our current
confusions. They need not do so. I do not think that national,
regional, cultural or political integrity are seriously threatened by the
growth of a united Europe or that any particular legal or
constitutional invention need of itself cause this erosion. The agreed
and shared adoption of a single market by 1993 will no more

eradicate the Frenchness of the French or the Englishness of the English than the nineteenth-century *Zollverein* (customs union) caused Bavarians or Prussians to shed their particular qualities and characteristics. On the other hand, we are undoubtedly seeing a degree of progressive Europeanisation, partly at the expense of national and local differences, that it would be myopic to deny.

As I travel in Western Europe, I am increasingly struck, and in general favourably impressed, by the confident common culture I see emerging. I do not mourn the way our Spanish neighbours have sloughed off the *mañana* image in a bid to cross commerce with culture, or the way the Italians nowadays vie with the French as world fashion leaders. And I applaud the way England, once a *Land ohne Musik* (land without music), now hosts a quite bewilderingly cosmopolitan musical life. As the bankers of Barcelona and Frankfurt flash English-language messages to each other, while their children fly across to Paris or London as students or *au pairs*, a truly common culture is emerging. Old-fashioned nationalism is on the wane: not (and this is my point) primarily because of the economic internationalists in Brussels, but because of far deeper trends in our shared history. The development of air transport, of electronic means of instant communication, and of the mass production of styles of food, clothing and architecture have had far more impact upon the growth of a shared European culture than regulations about apples and mutton and butter and wine.

Whether all this will lead to a new European nation seems to me a separate question. A shared culture is one thing; a shared government another. For all our communal political values, the much-vaunted erosion of national sovereignties embodied in NATO, the Common Agricultural Policy and so on, I do not see a United States of Europe coming together in the near future. For one thing, no government voluntarily gives up part of its power easily, let alone twelve such governments. More profoundly, new nations have always, I think, come into existence aggressively, usually after fighting *against* someone, overthrowing or escaping from a previous system, seceding from other nations like the thirteen American colonies, fighting off a larger nation as in the case of Italy or Algeria, reclaiming ancient lands, as in the case of Israel, or resisting supposed enemies like the first French Republic after the Revolution. In other words, it would seem that hostility *against* something or someone is often a major component in the making of a new nation. All had to wrench their sovereignty from somebody else. It is as if the law of immunity applied to national organisms rather as it does to human bodies. Viability consists in overcoming an adversary. A sad and bizarre reflection? Perhaps, but I cannot for the moment think of any example of a new nation creating itself out of a purely positive impulse with no external resistance to fight against.

Does this mean that no eventual European nation is ever possible except as a result of conflict? Not necessarily. Europe would not be Europe if it were to fail to find a new way to cope with an old dilemma. It is this very capacity to forge novelty from a base of tradition that is so quintessentially European: a delicate link between the values of Burkean Britain, if you like, and Revolutionary France (a theme to which we will return in Chapter 10). In twentieth-century terms, we have to tread an equally delicate path between the First and Second World Wars neither clinging to an old-fashioned view of Europe as being a federation of nations (impotent like the League of Nations) nor stumbling into a new continental agglomeration controlled by a unitary political system. The absolute sovereignty of the nation state is surely a thing of the past. But, as events in East Europe and all over the USSR daily remind us, so is the nightmarish Orwellian vision of a solid superbloc. One thing is certain. The new Europe cannot and will not materialise in a nineteenth-century way. It has to invent a new process, a new way of coping with itself. Perhaps the Founding Fathers of the European Community did after all have something to fight against: any possible recurrence of the clash of nationalisms that broke out in 1914 or of the even more apocalyptic clash of moral systems a generation later.

We will not get far if we think in purely territorial and political terms. The old question of how large an ideal unit of political sovereignty should be has never been satisfactorily answered. More fruitful, I think, is a cultural approach to the problem. Perhaps we should talk of the emergence of a number of overlapping *sub*-cultures that between them provide the warp and weft of the Europe of the future: the young athletes and musicians who criss-cross the continent, a rapidly expanding business network, long-distance lorry drivers who meet for a *demi* or a pint all along the motorways of Europe; and, of course, writers and academics such as myself, at home wherever their learning and their linguistic skills take them. The youngsters in their jeans and sweatshirts, the businessmen with their multi-lingual conference calls, the truck drivers, the academics and poets: few now think in the narrow national terms of their forebears. Their frame of reference is at once smaller and larger than the nation state. It is smaller in that it is often limited to people rather like themselves. Our world is full of academics, for example, who are only really comfortable in the presence of other academics, journalists who seek out fellow journalists, and so on. But these links very often stretch far beyond traditional national boundaries, too, as the bankers, jewellers, teachers, hoteliers, priests and poets of Barcelona and Birmingham, Munich and Milan, Lisbon and Lyon link hands across old animosities often almost ignoring the national capitals which still try to keep them under control.

We live in a privileged time, a watershed in history that invites or obliges us to rethink our identity and redefine notions about politics, sovereignty and the nation state which we have been in danger of taking for granted. Northern France is in many ways a good place to start. For centuries this part of Europe was the most criss-crossed network of commerical routes and fairs, the liveliest area for human exchanges before the blight of nationalism set in and the fighting by which it was accompanied. We have to re-cross the Somme back through its history, asking questions as we go: Why is it, for example, that the concept of the 'nation', once largely linguistic and cultural in meaning, came to freeze into territorial units? We have to ask whether the idea of the nation is not in contradiction to that of democracy, and whether the boost to nationalism which emanated from the French Revolution was in the long run really so beneficial. Why is it that the concept of democracy is only applied within political regimes and not across them? What effects on sovereignty would be incurred by the genuine application of democracy across national boundaries? Historically democratic nations have often themselves been nationalistically expansive and military, taking their cue perhaps from the French Revolution, which in the name of the people cried

Vive la Nation!, placed the people under arms, and embarked upon an imperialstic rampage across the map of Europe. France and Britain, pioneers of democracy, went on to be the great colonial conquerors.

In other words, the notion of sovereignty seems to have been linked with the old feudal notion of territoriality. It is as if our modern democratic nation states had blindly and unconsciously carried along with them into the modern age those feudal notions, worsening their effects immeasurably by coupling them with the idea of a 'democratic' army. All this, culminated in the First World War, a mass slaughter which brought together the essentially medieval concept of territoriality, nineteenth-century nationalism and the emerging ideal of mass democracy. Those cold, dead bodies, lying in their half-forgotten graves: what bearing should they have, or do they have, on the Europe of today and tomorrow? Did those poor soldiers die believing in national frontiers that are soon to be lifted? Or did they die precisely in order that their eventual descendants might raise those barriers and thus avoid such internecine slaughter in the future?

If we can come up with imaginative answers to questions such as these, answers appropriate for a future beyond memory of two world wars, then perhaps the men lying beneath the crosses of the Somme might not have died in vain. We owe it to them, and to ourselves therefore, to re-cross that small Rubicon of the north, for rivers are but barriers in the mind.

7

Out of the Trench

They are soon to open a Museum of the First World War in Picardy. The place chosen for the site lies slightly east of the Somme battlefields, in Péronne. Of course they had to think of the comfort and convenience of the potential visitors, some of whom might be more attracted to the battlefields of the Somme if they could be comforted at night by a jollier show, which means proximity to Paris. So they selected a place by the motorway that links Paris to Germany via Belgium and to England via the Channel. Tourists of the First World War can thus take in the whole show at one gulp, replenishing their emotions along with their fuel tanks.

I do not wish to sound cynical. Such a museum was long overdue. In the years immediately after the conflict a state of ennui and inertia set in which helps to explain why the French did not think of opening some form of museum earlier. What they did instead was to give each fighting nation its own piece of land for the burial of its dead and/or for the erection of an individual monument. Thus the road that runs from Albert to Bapaume, then on to Arras and Lens, north-east of Amiens, is on either side virtually one vast cemetery for fifty kilometres or more. Here are buried – by the hundred or by the thousand – Scots and Welshmen, New Zealanders and Australians, Canadians and Ulstermen, Chinese and Indians, Englishmen from the north and Englishmen from the south. The cemeteries are of various shapes and sizes. Some are just neat rows of crosses or of identical stone tombs surrounded by sloping green swards dotted by the occasional cluster of poppies. Here and there an exotic cedar or spruce shadows the graves. These great plots of peace are almost invisible in the midst of huge expanses of French farmland that once resounded with the ceaseless clamour of mechanised destruction. Except for the locals tending the wheat and barley that nod in the breeze in the summer time, the French rarely stop along this route. It is as though we were living a collective amnesia. By the time the Second World War erupted, indeed, the French at least had already almost wilfully forgotten the First.

French neglect of the First World War was little short of scandalous. The massacres of Picardy and Flanders were almost too brutal to think about, and a certain communal amnesia was understandable. But it contributed, I think, to the total lack of preparedness in France to face war again in 1939 and 1940. You may not *like* to think about the catastrophe you have had to endure, but ignoring it does not help equip you to avoid another.

There is a deeper reason, I think, over and above the sheer horror of the war of the trenches, why the French tended to ignore the First World War. We pride ourselves on being a literary nation. Anything major in our history had, by definition, to be immortalised by great writers, particularly poets. But who of note wrote of the First World War? If there is a literary tradition arising out of the death and destruction along the Somme it is not French but British: Siegfried Sassoon, Wilfred Owen, Isaac Rosenberg, Ivor Gurney and the rest, poets whose names mean little in France. My schoolboy memories from the 1950s are that on 11 November we would file past the local *Monument aux Morts* , an ugly piece of unsculpture erected in front of the village church. There, in the drizzle of a grey afternoon, we would sing the *Marseillaise* and then, on the stuttering orders of the local mayor, observe one minute's silence. Having complied we were rewarded with a cup of hot chocolate served in the nearest café; and that was that.

My interest in the First World War arose elsewhere. I grew up knowing that my father had been orphaned at the age of four, his own father having been cut to smithereens in an infamous wood called *Le Bois de la Gruerie*. As a result my father's life had been shattered. His mother had remarried and he had fled from home and been raised by relatives. Twenty-five years later, war ruined his life a second time as he was imprisoned by the Germans in Silesia for the duration of the Second World War. My father is really a double casualty of Europe's folly in the twentieth century. On my mother's side, one uncle, whose portrait my grandmother hung religiously on her bedroom wall, had been killed carrying soup and meat to the front lines. All this I knew as a small child. And I remember, too, the *Larousse Encyclopaedia of the Great War* in my grandparents' bookcase. From this I learned history and reading at one and the same time. Years later at university I switched my allegiance as a graduate from Greek and Latin to the study of English Literature, and when I had to write a master's dissertation I chose as my topic the English War Poets.

I had to work on my dissertation alone. The English War Poets were not on the Paris syllabus. Not only were they not French but they also rubbed salt into a peculiarly French wound, that of the French artistic talent meaninglessly wasted by the war: Charles Péguy, Jacques Rivière, Alain Fournier, Gaudier-Brzeska, and so on. To my teachers in Paris, no major work of art in any field had been produced by the war, with the possible exceptions of works such as Barbusse's *Under Fire* or Céline's *Journey to the End of the Night* (though this was more a general indictment on the century's materialism than a response to the First World War as such).

The real artistic movement of the period – Modernism – had nothing to do with the First World War and indeed predated its outbreak by several years. Already Picasso and Braque were experimenting with Cubism, while Matisse and Kandinsky were freeing colour from line. Stravinsky followed the lead of Debussy, adding savage rhythmic vitality to subtle orchestral texture, while the Dadaists in Zurich were taking poetry in directions unimaginable to the nineteenth-century formalists against whom they were rebelling. Thus to the French the War, when it came in 1914, was in aesthetic terms at least an almost supernumerary event breaking out anachronistically after the real upheaval had already taken place. It would certainly uproot lives, but it added no ideas.

If the War was largely disregarded in France in the 1920s and 1930s, it was virtually erased from people's minds by the Second World War which was to give rise to a new and far more troubled set of literary and artistic associations: Malraux dropping literature for war and going off to fight in an armoured division, Brasillach fraternising with the Germans and a younger generation of thinkers – Camus, Sartre – retrospectively examining their consciences for not having been involved earlier and more diligently in the fight against the Nazis. Thus by the time I came to write my dissertation on the English poets of the First World War, I was utterly out of touch with the time and place in which I lived.

The Modernism so dominant in France had left England almost untouched. England was an island fortress of tradition that not even a crusading American like Ezra Pound bent on catching up with progress in art had managed to budge. Standing aloof from aesthetic movements on the continent, England's most revered literary figures, such as Thomas Hardy or Arnold Bennett, continued to write in an essentially nineteenth-century tradition as though oblivious of the surge of Modernism flowing all around them. Much the same was true in other arts. Elgar, Holst and Vaughan Williams did not learn much from Debussy or Ravel, and neither did Stanley Spencer or Walter Sickert learn as much as they might have from Braque and Picasso. Indeed the War Poets did not seem touched by Rimbaud or Mallarmé. So how should they be judged? Not an easy question for a young Frenchman to answer when I first faced it in my dissertation thirty years ago. As war heroes? Surely not. As artists? Well, it may have sounded unappreciative of a foreigner to say so, but I could not resist the thought that they were prized above all as martyred bastions of anti-Modernism.

This is where France and England part company in their assessment of art. The French tend to analyse their artists in the context of the aesthetic movements of which they formed a part; the English, more emotionally, love to link an artist's life to his art (hence the great success of literary biographies in the English-speaking world). And what could be more emotion-laden than a group of talented poets who wrote, and in some cases died, on a foreign field of battle? But what about art? How does their poetry compare not just with that of their continental contemporaries, but with the more innovative English language models available to them, such as the work of Gerard Manley Hopkins or Ezra Pound? And was not T.S. Eliot in his *Waste Land* to bury them with more compassion than they could master in their own fight for survival? 'The poetry is in the pity', exclaimed Wilfred Owen in one of his most memorable pronouncements. Yet I cannot help detecting in Owen and the others a plea to the reader not only for sympathy for their plight as warriors but also for pity towards the inevitable inadequacies of the poetry itself.

Strangely enough the least considered of the War Poets and the best by any artistic standard was a survivor. Did he pay the penalty for that? Did he fail to qualify because among the requirements for being a celebrated War Poet was that one should have been killed? Or was it because besides being a survivor he was also a Welshman and, worse still, a Catholic? David Jones's *In Parenthesis* was published by Faber in 1937 and preceded by a lengthy preface by Eliot himself. Like Céline's novel, Jones's poem was a delayed reaction to the catastrophe. He had taken time to digest the thing and pieced together a *chef d'oeuvre*, a transcendent view of man and war in the tradition of Blake. But most of the War Poets, certainly those who died in the War, retained an innocent, almost bucolic English insularity in their work; an aesthetic equivalent, perhaps, of those cricketers a generation later who, bowling each other out for fun on the summery lawns of England, were shortly to be bowled out for ever by Death.

The traditional spirit of safe, stolid, rural England had managed to survive almost unimpaired throughout the Industrial Revolution, certainly among the moneyed classes. Even the most virulent attacks against aspects of the rural idyll shared fundamentally similar values and were launched by revivalists rather than radicals. I have in mind a writer like D H Lawrence in *The Rainbow*, published in 1916 and immediately suppressed by censorship. Through the character of Ursula, Lawrence protested against nationalistic values in the name of the eternal laws of Nature. His tracts were *Tintern Abbeys* revisited, as were Hardy's, deploring in the name of all that was old, honest and rural the traps laid in the path of Jude. I suspect that what the English like so much about their War Poets is the image they suggest of the English themselves, standing innocently poised on the eve of the twentieth century, at the very moment when the countryside spirit was to be obliterated forever by the destructive power of modern mass industrialism.

In this light it becomes easier to see why the Somme means so much more to the British than to the French. It is not only that the French, for their own often disreputable reasons, have chosen to ignore the First World War almost from the moment of its conclusion; in addition, the British have very strong reasons to remember that War and to envelop it in a cloud of almost romantic nostalgia. Nowhere is this better exemplified than in the famous 'Roses of Picardy', a song written by an Englishman at rest behind the front-lines and which, to the French – always hard to please and little convinced that roses could ever grow in the rain-drenched fields of Picardy – has always sounded morbidly exotic, conjuring up visions of blood drops passing for petals.

The English elevated the War with poetry while the French dealt with it, if at all, in prose, perhaps prosaically (with the exception of Apollinaire, who found excitement rather than depression in the artillery; his *Calligrammes* reflect the pure aestheticism which has always been part of the French aristic tradition). Blaise Cendrars in *La Main Coupée* mixes pity, humour and heroism in a way reminiscent of his German counterpart Ernst Jünger in *The Storm of Steel* and it comes as no surprise to read Robert Graves reporting in *Goodbye to All That* how his friend Sassoon declared wearily: 'Please, no more war,' – then suddenly, animatedly – 'except against the French!'

In spite of the *entente cordiale* there were no two countries more unlike in Europe than Britain and France at the time. England enjoyed (if that is the right word) a longer, slower emergence, or descent, from the nineteenth-century than France. In France, the twentieth-century had already arrived well before 1914 . In Britain it struck, finally and forcibly, in 1940. But let me not sound complacent. My impression is that we are still, all of us, standing at low water, having pinned our values for so long on our national identities and only now coming to realise that the blood wasted on nationhood can no longer glue the picture together. Through the mask of Prufrock Eliot asked which mask should we wear now?

Saying *Goodbye to All That* to retire on the Spanish isle of Majorca, Robert Graves spent his life pitting (as he wrote so excitingly in *The White Goddess*) 'feminine' values of Love against 'masculine' values of War. He does not seem to have been heard or followed by his countrymen. Perhaps he still drew too much on the aristocratic values that had prevailed before the disaster. Perhaps courtly love is still too enmeshed with the warlike values of conquest. On the French side André Breton hinged Surrealism on the pivot of *amour fou* (mad love) in the name of which he conducted a literary war with casualties, suicides and exclusions. Still very much a game of masculine power vying for a prize! Have we learned nothing from two world wars? The aesthetic legacy suggests not. The essentially national values that led to the wars have not been replaced by a larger literary vision. At best, acid protests have been made (Beckett, Ionesco, Cioran) and derisive games have been played (Joyce, Robbe-Grillet, Perec). The shattering echo is still with us. Indeed many people still seem readier to leap to arms than to link them.

This has been a sombre essay in a book essentially optimistic. British readers may take exception to my strictures on the hallowed War Poets, though I have hardly been more complimentary to the French literary tradition. Or perhaps my very criticisms are a kind of compliment; for I profoundly believe the poet must have a voice and a vision – as Eliot did, as David Jones did – that will lead us beyond present discontents. It is not enough for art to regret the passing of values that are no longer helpful, and worse if art works to perpetuate them. I am not against the establishment of a Museum of the Somme and condemn utterly the French disease of amnesia regarding the First World War. But let us remember that War as the graveyard of the nationalism that produced it, and give a decent burial once and for all to the outmoded values its wretched combatants had to espouse and for which so many of them died.

8

Home Sweet Home!

I was brought up near the Somme and as a young teenager I attended the Lycée at Abbeville. I was still very much a provincial in those days, almost oblivious of the implications of the global conflict from which we had recently emerged. I knew little of politics or world affairs. My life was wrapped up in scholarly obligations such as leaving the house in the village where we lived at 7 o'clock every morning to moped eight miles up the road to school. I can still see myself dressed like a visitor from an alien planet bent over his machine to face the strong winds blowing in from the sea. Of school itself I remember little, except that it bored me. My life was in the wider spaces, in the sheer fact of being alive and in touch through my senses with the fields and the sky and sea beyond. I used to think I was following in the tracks of millions of my predecessors throughout history as, daily, I re-enacted their ambivalent progress from village to town, from happy rural ignorance to the dubious benefits of urban learning.

My mind and body were attuned to the elements around me, and to the seasons, and it was these rather than an academic knowledge of history that tied me to my ancestors with a link both binding and flexible. I came from a long chain of anonymous peasant farmers who had been left largely unworried by history except in periods of famine. Even the recent war had left people in that part of Picardy with a sense of humour and of the relativity of things.

Our village in the Forest of Crécy was adjacent to the launching-pads of the V-1s targeted on London, and local lore was full of tales of those flying weapons boomeranging on themselves erratically,

71

killing their launchers (and maybe us). I remember a quick-witted local peasant woman at the farm where my mother bought eggs and butter each weekend, a strong-breasted, round-bodied woman, with immense charm in her apparent ugliness. She told us of the RAF bombardments which had flattened her beautiful house and attendant barns. One night, she said, she ventured back to her gutted farmhouse just to gaze through its holed roof at the eternal starry sky above. This bossy old peasant woman spoke in almost visionary tones, calmly, beautifully, convinced that to have been left alive after such a disaster was a sufficient grace. As I listened to the fatalism and good humour her voice conveyed, I cast a silent vote once and for all for poetry over politics.

Yet politics existed all around us. It boomed from the wireless set as we heard about world-wide Communist aggression, the Berlin Airlift, the role of France as linchpin in the Western Alliance. All this angered my parents. My father had fought in the infantry in 1940, been demobbed by Pétain, then rounded up by the local Pétainist mayor as a Prisoner of War destined for a German labour camp. My childhood had been lulled by his censored letters trickling out from far-away Silesia, and food parcels which my mother sent and which miraculously reached him and fuelled his longing for France. At the end of the War his camp was behind Russian lines and it was they who liberated him. When finally he returned and I met my father for virtually the first time, the person I encountered was angry, depressed; and a man who would not hear a word said against the Russians throughout the Cold War years that followed. How could I be oblivious of politics in such an atmosphere? Slowly it dawned on my lazy political consciousness that after the War was — war: in Korea, Palestine, India, and (for France) in Indo-China and Algeria. The seeds of these conflicts had been sown in previous generations, but the killing was being done today. I remember feeling that war is essentially an old-fashioned affair and that it stinks of previous centuries, even when fought with modern weapons.

In many respects our century, the twentieth, is but an annex, a footnote to the nineteenth. Europe, though divided since Yalta, is collectively the legatee of essentially nineteenth-century ideas: for example, the extraordinary notion of progress through rivalry, loosely referred to as Social Darwinism, that has been the basic common frame of reference for Western liberalism and Soviet Marxism alike. The notion of progress came into its own as Europe gradually divested itself of the centuries-old notion of a finite eternal universe created as such by God. In our own time, the idea of 'progress' has lost much of its moral content and been increasingly equated with the idea of 'change' and thereby, perhaps, the elevation of ends over the nature of the means: Machiavellism redrafted by Doctor Frankenstein!

A second product of the nineteenth century that has shaped our experience of the twentieth is nationalism. This too derives indirectly from the breaking of traditional bonds. Nationalism is essentially Protestant; it stems from the protest voiced by dissenters against the blindly unintelligent version of the Gospels given out by the Catholic Church. The protest was at first linguistic; historians often underrate the part played by Luther and Calvin as translators. From linguistic nationalism — that is the right of access to the Bible in one's own tongue — state nationalism gradually followed. England's Henry VIII went to his grave regarding himself a Catholic, but not a *Roman* Catholic. It was the Church of England, and thereby the idea of the *nation* of England, that his protest helped to forge. In France the idea of nationhood did not fully emerge until the Revolution displaced both monarchy and church. 'Vive la Nation!' cried the revolutionaries at Valmy, swinging their caps on the tips of their upturned swords: '*la Nation* — that is — *en armes*. At the dawn of the nineteenth-century, therefore, the ideas of protest and progress linked arms, and were joined enthusiastically by militant nationalism.

How far have we, 200 years later, progressed from that idea of progress? I sometimes feel that, like Darwinian rats or Pavlovian dogs, we are still caught in the trap (or maze) of 'progress through nationalism', unable to find a way out. Mind you, I also think we are still stuck in even earlier attitudes, pre-Protestant as it were. I was recently invited to attend a seminar in Brussels on the question, 'Is there a European *Imaginaire*?' I had to deliver my paper early on the first day when minds and spirits were not yet quite keyed to the occasion and my paper had the unintended but revealing effect of setting imaginations at war. I was heckled mercilessly. I sounded too poetic, too metaphorical (some critics sniffed). Worse, I had spoken openly of religious matters, and even gone to the extent of pronouncing the name of God in the Université Libre de Bruxelles, which I had thought to be the non-confessional Belgian university *par excellence*, as opposed to Catholic Louvain. These reactions shocked me. I grew up in a society predominantly Catholic but containing a strong lay tradition. In Belgium, religion was evidently still a political issue. I thought back to my early adolescence, cycling my youthful way past the early morning fields glistening with dew. Could politics be so all-pervasive? I had not been able to believe this then, and I still could not do so now. Everything is political if you define the word loosely enough. And yet, if you retain a larger perspective, nothing is. A paradox? It is one that as a poet I am happy to live with and one I wish our political leaders would have the courage to emulate.

Can whole societies share the inconsistencies of a poem and contain in themselves as much uncertainty as certainty, as much openness towards the unknown as protection from any unwelcome effects? In facing those questions, politicians are the great rivals of poets. They make poetry that works, they say, poetry that moves crowds, that sums up a whole story for millions of people in a neat capping phrase. Some of the great political utterances of history, (Churchill's war-time speeches, for example), were in their way the work of a poet. In our own day, someone like Mikhael Gorbachev, struggling with the inconsistent pressures to which he himself has given encouragement, endeavours to encapsulate paradox within a single speech. But what does he mean when he refers to the Europe of tomorrow as our 'common home'? In French we have only one word, *maison*, to mean both house and home, where English distinguishes between the external structure and the intimate interior. Which has President Gorbachev in mind? And what kind of shared accommodation can he mean, speaking as he does as the leader of a country, many of whose constituent elements are even now trying to leave his Soviet home and set up house separately?

If there is to be a new *maison commune* it must be a beginning, not an end. A child will draw a house as a first drawing, or perhaps himself or herself inside a house, but that child will soon venture outside. And I still can't help worrying slightly when I see Europe viewed as a house by somebody who comes from a region where, historically at least, they have usually built better jails than houses. We are here on earth not only to build houses or even to turn them into homes and raise families within them. We have to be free to venture out of them, beyond home and hearth, to embark upon our personal voyage unimprisoned by our place of initial residence. Politicians, even enlightened ones, too often try to restrict. It is poetry that insists on liberation.

'Let's go out of this world, anywhere, be it to Hell!' expostulates Baudelaire at the end of 'Le Voyage'. If Europe is to achieve a new shared identity, it will have to jettison those fundamentally nineteenth-century values of progress through nationalism which it first acquired and then spread throughout the world as it lost its colonies. We need to develop a new concept of 'home' − not a *narrow*, restrictive one, but an idea that links security with adventure, the fixed with the fluid, territory with travel, poetry with politics.

9

Rivers of Time

The face of London is changing. The banks of the Thames are being redeveloped. Soon the Globe Theatre will resume its activities as in Shakespeare's time. One literary age expels another. The London that is passing away is that of Dickens. Twenty years ago it was still possible to glimpse the world of Fagin and Bill Sykes, and to visualise Pip in *Great Expectations* as he tried to spirit the convict Magwitch to the continent, sneaking through the huge, forbidding barges, and taking advantage of the tide. When I first used to visit London in the early 1960s, one could still stroll down the Embankment and smell the scents of cinnamon and pepper floating down from the pulley-equipped lofts of the East or West India Docks. This was the exotic London, with its pungent colonial flavour, that inspired French poets such as Pierre Mac Orlan (a Picard in spite of his Irish name) who wrote evocatively of Limehouse Causeway. London had the advantage over Paris, for it was a colossal harbour directly linked to the whole world.

Literature is the best guide to a town because it gives you enhanced access to reality. One needs that little extra spice of fiction to make reality more savoury. I remember spending a whole day tracing the route followed by the 'carbuncular clerk' of the *Waste Land*, alias T.S. Eliot, drifting from St Mary Woolnoth's down King's Road to Lower Thames Street in order to catch intimations of the post-1918 gloom that still haunts the City, its monuments and its stones. But perhaps the writer who made me love London best, especially that vanishing, colonial, maritime London, is the Polish exile, Joseph Conrad. How appropriate that his stories flow through the narration of a figure named (after the Thames-side town?) Marlow. Who can forget Marlow, aboard a ship at anchor on the river across Greenwich, waiting for the tide to turn? The tale he is to unfold is a tale of horror, of crime and punishment. Yet, for me, it has placed its permanent seal on the city, has cast such a spell that I can never think of London and its river except through Marlow's – or Conrad's – expectant eyes. For Conrad evoked, as perhaps only an outsider could, the colour, the exoticism, the dirt and ultimately the destructiveness of London's colonial economy.

Conrad's London, like that of Dickens, is a thing of the past. 'Le petit Paris' (dear little old Paris), wrote Charles Baudelaire, 'n'est plus'. And he might well have said the same of London, even then. But what would Baudelaire or Dickens or Conrad – let alone Shakespeare – make of the Thames-side developments of the new London that is emerging? How would they write of the vast new plateglass city which disingenuously pretends to gain inspiration from the docks it so blatantly replaces? Or of the busloads and light railway loads of tourists who come for a whiff of a rich history that the new 'Docklands' has utterly obliterated? The whole riverside used to teem with real activity and now exudes artifice. The river was once the essential life-blood of those who worked on and alongside it. Today it is regarded as at best a picturesque irrelevance. There was an awful irony in the tragic accident that occurred on the Thames on the night of 20 August 1989 when a dredger capsized a little pleasure boat killing many of the wealthy and beautiful young people who had been partying aboard. It was almost as though a clumsy, old, nearly obsolete species of animal, a carthorse perhaps, were kicking out one last time at the slick new generation by which it was being displaced. Here was Dickens's London avenging itself, it almost seemed, on the new London hard at work earning shallow money. The toll was heavy. But the Thames is a toll-river.

There was a further ironic twist in that the ill-fated pleasure boat had long ago helped British troops evacuate Dunkirk across the Channel before most of the unfortunate youngsters had been born. Thus this little vessel had itself graduated from an urgent mission to save lives in the midst of war to a leisurely life of pleasure brought abruptly to a brutal end in the midst of a party. A metaphor for

Britain's recent history? Or London's? And is there a deeper significance in the fact that London, after three centuries of development westwards, is returning to its origins (like the painters of the Forth Bridge) and redeveloping its time-worn eastern outposts? I do not know, although I hope the new Docklands scheme will not prove to be the prototype for the *next* three centuries of London development. As a frequent visitor from abroad I have the feeling that London is breaking loose once more from its moorings, and that the whole history-laden boat is floating freely on its great river seeking a new berth; perhaps closer to the Continent to which its destiny is increasingly drawn.

Let me not be unmitigatedly rude about Docklands, however. The new plateglass Utopia bespeaks a flamboyant new wealth that may sit ill alongside Wren's Greenwich or the working-class housing estates it dwarfs. But it does proclaim a kind of American or Japanese 'megabuck' wealth wholly in tune with its money-making ethos and vocation. The Docks, just as in Dickens's and Conrad's time, are on the move. Forget London the stately old capital city, they seem to say. Think of change, of the future, of the wider world to which we were always the link. London's greatness was always based on trade and finance. Its political power may have mesmerised historians, but this was always secondary, is certainly so now, and will recede even further in the larger Europe of the future. *This* is where power lies: raw, economic power! Joseph Conrad might even have approved.

He would certainly have noted a delicious irony in the fate of the Thames. The decline of rivers as commercial vectors, combined with the cleansing of their streams as demanded by ecologists, frees them from the murkier legacy of their history. Today, the Thames flows freely, 'superfluously', and people talk of salmon breeding in its waters. Is the Thames, Londoners ask, still the central artery of the capital's industrial wealth and power? Or should it be content merely to hose down and refresh the system? For the first time since the early Middle Ages, the Thames has lost its major industrial purpose, and has immediately been seen to benefit.

In Paris there is no parallel, and neither are Parisians animated by such debate. Paris was and is a continental town, and the small amount of commercial activity on the slow, lazy Seine was always placed away from the city. The river was, primarily, neither an industrial route nor a mere ecological fancy, but a High Street, fully integrated into the city planning as though built to reflect the monuments that line its banks. Indeed, since the time of Georges Pompidou, a lover among lovers of the Paris heritage (and a banker by training, open to modernisation and investment), the Seine has harboured on its banks several expressways destined to mop up the overflow of cars and reflect even more precisely the flow of the river they accompany.

Historically, the closer a river city was to the sea the better. London or Glasgow had advantages denied to Paris or Lyon. Today, however, a great river is often mere decoration, a waterfront. I remember the first time I saw the Mississippi at New Orleans. Such a narrow embankment for so grand a flow of water! It was as though the river itself had contracted in order to become more amenable to those who chose to stare at it. For centuries the history of entire continents was shot through with the literally vital question of the accessibility of their principal cities to the sea. Remember, for instance, the historic importance to the Russians of Archangel or to the Spaniards of Seville, or how the city of Bruges was challenged by the ascendancy of Antwerp. London's wealth and fortune grew from its miraculous poise between sea and fresh water. Now the map of power is changing again, and is being redesigned for other routes and axes of power.

If some of the great rivers of the world – the Thames, the Rhine, the Mississippi – are losing much of their former significance, those most likely to survive these changes with their dignity intact are the small, unpretentious streams least worn by the demands of history. I think, for example, of the tiny river in northern France near which I was born, the Maye, which flows through Crécy and loses itself in the Channel, a mere fifty kilometres away. The Maye became my personal silver thread, leading me through the scattered fragments of my life, giving them ease and flow and consistency. Through its reflection, I came to reflect on my relation to Time: that is, both rhythmic time as a poet, and existential time as a human being. Such rivers have retained their original liquidity as they surge towards nowhere, one of the last and most authentic manifestations of the abundance of Nature. As such they are like poetry: a garrulity of the soul, a *bavardage* (babbling) of life, a breathing of Time in its earthly continuity. Yet rivers are not shallow, as poetry is sometimes thought to be by very serious people too busy to pay attention to it; for they have the depth of Time made transparent to itself. For the West, for Western Europe and America, which have contributed so much towards the exploitation and exhaustion of animal and mineral resources throughout the world, even our tiniest rivers present a chance for reflection, wisdom and meditation. They have continued to flow through and beyond the ravages of Time. But will we?

This, surely is the message of our poets and their frequent and loving references to that symbol of continuity, rivers: the Wye, which falls alongside Wordsworth's Tintern Abbey and whose very name seems to reflect a muted question; or the tumultuous bull-necked beck, rushing a few miles from Basil Bunting's Briggflatts in Cumbria, a river called Rawthey.

> Brag sweet tenor bull
> Descant on Rawthey's madrigal,
> Each pebble its part
> In the Fell's late spring

Or consider the poetic evocations of American rivers, continuity in the very land of 'Now' and 'Here': the organ-voiced Mississippi in T.S. Eliot's *Four Quartets*; William Carlos Williams's Passaic River, leaping and bounding over Paterson, New Jersey; or Whitman's Hudson reflecting not dawns but dusks as the sun dies over Manhattan. Rivers, so many rivers, the visible images of the timelessness of time on earth.

By the banks of the Shannon at Clonmacnoise in Ireland was erected a monastery that became, in effect, the first European university of repute and strength. There, on a hillock rising above a bend in the river, one can imagine the *scriptoria* or copyists busily turning out their manuscripts, aided by the mildness of the climate, the abundance of fish in the river and the comforting presence of the elder sages lying in their tombs. The excitement of learning combined with the peace of Nature is surely a goal worth attaining. I have such a dream for the European university of the future where our latter-day *scriptoria* would produce twenty-first-century equivalents of the Book of Kells: high-definition videos, perhaps, reflecting lasting truths and resulting from long exposure to the ancient lore that has preceded them. A fantasy? Possibly; for how can we reconcile the impetus and energy that fuel modern learning with a renewed sense of the deep continuities of time that link us to our own distant past? Some modern universities, mainly American, have tried to make that link by applying the latest techniques to the oldest disciplines. Teachers, certainly at university level, might be said to represent the permanence and continuity of knowledge, at least to successive generations of students each flying off to their various appointed stations in life.

In fact the message from most university teachers is, rather, that present-day society is no longer impressed by traditional learning. Greek, Latin, History, Philosophy: these are of no value alongside Business, Computing or Management Studies. Form is valued over content, technique over substance, modernity over tradition. It is almost as though a deliberate policy were being adopted of *dis*continuity with the past, a direct denial of the traditional role of the teacher as bridge between the generations. Indeed, learning as increasingly defined today scarcely needs a teacher as such. Today's skills can often be acquired in front of a computer terminal, which may be why teachers continue against the evidence to deny the crisis they themselves have helped to generate.

Perhaps we should dispense with teachers, at least in their mechanical role as transmitters of facts and skills. But let us not dispense with them altogether, for they have an essential role in any society: the teacher is the embodiment of the flow and continuity of Time, the representative to the young of the wisdom of the old, the encapsulation not only of fact but of value, of the flower of learning and of its deepest roots. The accumulated wisdom of mankind continues to flow, like a river, regardless of what one generation or another happens to erect or destroy on its banks. Those who plumb its depths, the poets and writers and seers, have a duty to speak out and to address the widest audiences they can reach, as the prophets of old or the *scriptoria* of the Middle Ages were not ashamed to do.

Perhaps we could start by building the new universities of the future on the banks of the River of Time.

10

Channel of History

We are on the beach at Calais, not far from the place where the cross-Channel ferries dock today. From the luminosity of the sky it seems we are in mid-summer. The sea is its usual sandy-brown, with just the occasional fleck of glassy-green atop the waves. There are not many people around, except perhaps a few shrimp-girls bending provocatively over the sand: those same trim girls that will later excite the painter Joseph Turner once the gates of Europe are reopened.

A man is strolling on the beach, holding a child by the hand. He is in his early thirties and the child about nine. Evidently they are talking in a very emotional way together, though it is hard to be sure which language they are using. Perhaps it is French, perhaps English, maybe a mixture of the two. The child, a little girl, has been brought up in Blois in France by a royalist family, but she is now meeting her real father for the first time. He is an English poet who had fled the French Revolution and gone back to live in his birth-place in the Lake District. He adores children who, he believes, are nature's true philosophers and able to peer into the depths of experience. Later, he will compose a poem on this particular evening, not one of his best, but the circumstances are fraught with enough emotion to make us listen:

> It is a beauteous evening, calm and free,
> The holy time is quiet as a Nun
> Breathless with adoration; the broad sun
> Is sinking down in its tranquillity.

The poet is of course William Wordsworth and the date August 1802, a few months after a temporary peace has been signed at Amiens between the French and the English. The child is Caroline, Wordsworth's child by Annette Vallon.

It is not too fanciful, I think, to take this stroll of a father and his estranged daughter on the beach at Calais in the lull of the Napoleonic storm as an evocative symbol of the estrangement of Europe from itself. In 1789, France had started a Revolution that not only cut it off from its neighbours but also wrenched it from its own roots, its own past. France reinvented itself, claiming to be a totally new nation-state, with a new legitimacy based on the ideas of Law and Nation instead of the King; a new religion, the worshipping of the Supreme Being; a new calendar, the Republican calendar where saints are replaced by seasons. But this pretension to novelty had been strongly opposed by all the old monarchies surrounding France: Austria, Prussia and, above all, England where political legitimacy lay not in innovation but in the Burkean concept of continuity.

This estrangement is still with us; the gap has still not been fully bridged. As we find ourselves on the eve of entering a new Europe where barriers are to be lifted, the French cannot quite understand why other nations, and in particular the British, seem to resist the opportunity to create something new out of past values. There are two forms of nationalism at loggerheads here, two diverging sensibilities, two philosophical conceptions. The French brought into the world – or first gave real currency to – the idea of Novelty as a value, while the English retained faith in their concept of Continuity. The fundamental question to which the eruption of the French Revolution gave enormous new impetus, therefore, concerned the respective merits of novelty and continuity, a debate which continues. Look, for instance, at the controversy in the arts – particularly architecture – between the proponents and opponents of Modernism. Or at the debate that rages around every new electronic invention: whether calculators help or hinder the teaching of maths or whether television and video enhance or destroy the coherence of the family.

The problem with novelty is that it shifts with great rapidity from fact to value. Now and tomorrow become the daily dimensions of our consumer society; yesterday is, by definition, out of date. This breathless modernity reached its apogee in the 1968 movement in Paris and throughout the world that self-consciously tried to ape the French Revolution of 1789 and marry it to the immediacy of latter-day America. The soi-disant revolutionaries of 1968 wanted freedom; and they wanted it 'Right Now!'. Gratification was to be immediate and stringless, 'here' and 'now'. Thus, the United States came to represent the ideal meeting-ground for the concept of Novelty started by the French Revolution and the impatience largely engendered by the new economic abundance. The war-cry of 'Right Now' echoed in a crude way Walt Whitman's famous programme drafted a century earlier:

> I have heard what the talkers were talking,
> the talk of the beginning and the end.
> But I do not talk of the beginning or the end.
> There was never any more inception than there is now.

If everything has to be 'now' and 'here', nothing is of durable value. A more recent American poet, e.e. cummings, put the two words together. If something is 'Now, here' it is, essentially, 'Nowhere'. As the time that elapses between innovation, adoption and obsolescence becomes ever shorter, novelty of itself becomes a more and more valued commodity regardless of its nature. It is 'new', so it must be 'good'. Here, I think, we touch on one of the essential problems of our civilisation: a problem not only of philosophy but of spirit.

The problem of novelty dates its modern genesis, I have suggested, from the French Revolution, and the Revolutionary culture – and the Romantic reaction – that followed in its wake. This is why a poet like William Wordsworth, who embodied both, is still very much with us today. Wordsworth was among the first to acclaim the French Revolution and the sheer novelty it seemed to embody. He went to France, enjoyed his stay there and had a child by Annette Vallon. Then, with the coming of the Terror, he turned his back on the Revolution, forgot about Annette and their child, and sank back into reveries about the mythological past of Britain, walking across Salisbury Plain and going to Wales before finally settling down in the Lake District. Wordsworth was now in effect taking over the

Romantic mantle from Rousseau, substituting a spiritual for a social contract. Man, said Wordsworth, 'is a time creature, living in time and by time'. To the poet of these years, therefore, it is the sense of the continuity of existence, the great durabilities, that really matter. We have to renew the contract between the present and the past, he says: the past nourishing the present, which in its turn gives raw material to our memories of the past.

Yet, for all Wordsworth's rejection of the horrors of obsessive 'Hereness' and 'Nowness', he seems to have retained, perhaps unconsciously, many of the ideas of the French Revolution and, indeed, to have carried back from France some of the very notions he was consciously resisting. For Wordsworth, after all, the most glorious moment of life is childhood: the dawn of life was so much richer a quarry for him than evening or night. Man, he says, travels from dawn to the extinction of light. And the job of the poet is to recapture the vanishing light of early childhood, his early sense of the light of dawn, and carry it with him to illuminate his old age. The child is the true philosopher; the finest time of day is dawn. Thus, just like the French Revolution that he came to resist so much, William Wordsworth also came to value youthful ingenuity, fresh ideas, new beginnings. Poetry may be the act of reminiscing in tranquillity, but it is also nostalgia for 'the beginnings', for a time when disruptive dreams could drive a wedge between past and present.

> Whither is fled the visionary gleam?
> Where is it now, the glory and the dream?

Unlike Wordsworth, I have never been obsessed with sources and springs, with the new and discontinuous, with mornings and dawns. Neither do I lament for a lost origin or for a past childhood. I am less haunted by the brevity of life than by its length. What interests me above all is the prospect of our lives lengthening more and more, owing to the progress of the medical and social sciences. We are, perhaps without noticing it, witnessing a revolution in our sensibilities, moving away from dawns and mornings in order to reach for the more mature sands of evening and night. No longer do we thirst for novelty at any cost, but rather we are beginning to develop a new sense of our own duration and of how to deal with it.

This, to me, is where Europe, with its values forged by the passage of history, comes back into the picture. We cannot be content with post-industrial materialism, the instant gratification demanded by the French Revolutionaries and nowadays imported from the United States and Japan. I do not think that we in Europe can or should vie with those countries of the Now Here. Instead, we should explore how we might reconcile and perhaps transcend the values of Novelty (as stimulated and expanded by the French Revolution and by American materialism) and the values of Continuity (as traditionally espoused by the English). We cannot act as if we lived in a constantly regenerated present with no history to shape us or knowledge of death to temper our aspirations. Freedom? Yes. Now only? No. The trick is to link the revolutionary cry for individual *liberté* (which we in the West have gone far towards achieving) with a deeper awareness of the historical continuities that shape our social, collective fate.

We have a long way to go. The mainly individualistic gains brought by the French Revolution have led to nation-states that elevate massive, passive materialism to the forefront of their value system. Was it for this that millions fought and died in two world wars? The massacres in the trenches of Flanders, and later in the ovens of Belsen and Auschwitz, were after all largely perpetrated by nationalistic societies whose individual members back home on the whole had their fair share of material comfort.

It seems to me that the gradual, inexorable process of European unification presents us with a unique opportunity to remould our values, to create an almost Hegelian synthesis of the values of Novelty and Continuity, of the interests of the individual and of those of the wider society. I make no pretensions to prophecy; but that the societies or cultures of Europe, particularly Western Europe, are in many ways converging there can surely be no room for doubt. Whatever federal, confederal or national statutes and constitutions provide the letters of our future law, at a deeper level our destinies are inevitably and increasingly intertwined.

Before launching into the Europe of tomorrow, therefore, before plunging into the creation of any kind of new multi-national nationalism, let us try to lay the foundations of a new spirituality that would perhaps graft the lay Trinity of the French Revolution — Freedom, Equality and Fraternity — on to the traditional Christian Trinity of Father, Son and Holy Ghost: the values of Novelty on to those of Continuity. The child is father of the man, wrote William Wordsworth, and the two should walk together, not in conflict. I too have stood on the sands at Calais, holding a little hand in my own, and strolled just along the beach from the entrance to what will be one of the most spectacular breaks with historical tradition we are likely to witness, the Channel Tunnel. This will of course be a tremendous feat of technology, linking Britain and France after literally centuries of dreaming. But the Tunnel will link two cultures which share a long history of mutual suspicion and antipathy. Will they, too, at last, be genuinely linked? Or will there remain two adjacent shores widely separated by the same truth? The danger for Europe would be that its dawn should reach night before having a chance to savour midday: that speedy, efficient modern technology will, as so often, present us with a tool for massive, instant communication before we have had time to assimilate the historical implication of what has become available. We need time as well as technology; tradition as well as modernity; Continuity as well as Novelty; Burke as well as the French Revolution. The New Europe must have a place for poetry as well as commerce, for spiritual as well as material values, for the parent as for the child as together they stroll towards a shared future.

11

Beyond Tintern

A decisive moment in European cultural history occurred when Wordsworth fled from the French Revolution that he had at first hailed and returned to his birth-place in the Lake District. In doing so he helped to anchor the national identity of England (and link it in part to the marvellous watery and mountainous country around Grasmere and Hawkshead) whilst the French, desperate to find harbour, went on to drift through ever-deeper waters. Wordsworthian England draws on its own roots in an almost organic cycle of renewal: here in its simplest and crudest form is the Protestant concept of Nation as force of Nature, soon to be expropriated by less innocent German philosophers. God is diffused throughout Nature and His law felt in every cloud and tree. The poet Basil Bunting, a Quaker, whom I visited in his Cumbrian redoubt many times before his death in 1985, continued nearly two centuries later to entertain a somewhat Wordsworthian view of things, an almost pantheistic equation of God with the immutable, organic forces of Nature. How different from the French Revolution which was bent only on uprooting the old order, marking a total divorce between Nature and Law and establishing a new transcendent system of man-made Law for which you were now expected to suffer and to die like an old Christian martyr.

To this day, British – especially English – nationalism is an organic nationalism of dissent, where each individual interiorises personally a social and political contract all presume to have the force of Nature. On the Continent, certainly in France, systems of law and politics are made by people and changeable by people. In English common law each case is considered as an offshoot of what preceded it, a new scion of an old legal bough, unlike the bureaucratic new laws that keep turning up tied in European red tape and postmarked Brussels. Indeed our respective nationalisms seem to me to carry the mark of a deeper, almost theological cleft.

In English Protestantism, everyone is to some extent his or her own priest. Wordsworth, indeed, used to conduct services with his co-celebrant (Dorothy) in the open just as John Wesley's Methodists had done *en masse* in countryside meadows. We French, on the other hand, traditionally needed prefects of the law just as the seasoned Catholics we are have always needed priests to put us in touch with the Divine mystery, incapable as it were of interiorising the natural law ourselves unaided. We needed prefects and priests to rail at, to be unruly against, and official screens behind which to shelter our deepest doubts.

Nowadays, apart from a small core of integrists, French Catholicism has developed a flexible, more individualistic approach towards Rome. The younger generation seem to respond to the notion of pilgrimage pronounced by Pope John Paul II at Santiago de Compostela, which combines a physically demanding goal to be attained in space (preferably on foot) with the notion of truth as being more of a protracted journey than an instant illumination. Now as then, however, French attitudes have been more outward-looking and less self-regarding than those of Protestant England, looking for illumination from above and beyond and explicitly expressed, rather than for implied messages from that by which one is immediately surrounded. And it was from the French to the English approach that Wordsworth retreated when settling down once more in the Lake District.

I prefer the journeying outwards to the journeying backwards of Wordsworth, not because I am a Frenchman but because I am a European, and because the time is long since past when one could retreat to one's birth-place as the greatest repository of truth and wealth. Why tie a 'place' to a 'birth'? The concept of a birth-place, a homeland, which has nourished European nationalism for the past two centuries, has done more evil than good, carrying as it does notions of territoriality and conquest, of segregation and exclusion.

It is not a question of *denying* one's roots or of avoiding the enrichment they can obviously bring. That would be foolish. The question rather is how to build on what they have to offer, to journey beyond them and not merely to treat them as a sanctuary within which to escape from a wicked world. Where should we start? Are there clues in Wordsworth himself? I wondered about this on a recent visit to Tintern Abbey. The Wye is greasy with pollution and the environment somewhat less sylvan than in Wordsworth's day. But the ruins of the Abbey remain a superb vision of an almost lost civilisation as they loom up so startlingly amongst the villages of the Welsh borders. Odd, perhaps, that Wordsworth spared no thought for the Cistercian origins of those ruins. Mind you, there is another church on the slope above Tintern, St Mary's, whose tower rises in the midst of a disused churchyard and overlooks a few comfortable new houses probably built by Bristol executives who commute daily between poetry and business. The entrance to St Mary's is blocked off with cemented bricks, so Catholicism is once again forgotten at Tintern. The English seem almost wilfully to forget that *all* their great ancient churches were monuments to Catholicism and that there was once a single religious force uniting the entire British Isles.

To me, Britain means *all* of Britain, not least — perhaps most of all — Celtic, Gaelic, pre-Roman Britain. My most recent visit to Tintern followed a trip to Ireland, once *the* home of European learning and enlightenment when so much else was plunged into darkness and war. If one is journeying in search of the roots of European culture, of our shared spiritual 'birth-place', a voyage across the Irish Sea can take us far beyond Tintern.

Ireland is a route rather than a destination, just as it was to James Joyce. Stephen Dedalus in *Ulysses* gets up and leaves his Martello Tower, his *Thoor Ballylee*, and sets off like some vagrant medieval Scot, some Saint Brendan of the waves, to pursue his personal odyssey to the truth. Joyce clearly believes there is no better place, no better birth-place, than the one we are travelling *towards*. The journey may end where it started; but what a wealth of experience is gathered *en route*!

Ireland provided a relatively late staging post in my own circuit. I had already travelled along several routes (not to say ruts) before coming to realise that the standard, set-piece tours through the European cultural tradition were not particularly to my taste. I felt ill at ease in the eighteenth-century spirit of pre-Revolutionary France which, for all its Voltairean brilliance, struck me as mainly a spirit of negation. I journeyed in the other direction, towards the romantic tradition. But we French have little authentic romanticism. Even with figures like Chateaubriand and Madame de Staël, theirs is essentially a derivative romanticism, English or German. So I found myself travelling back, all the time further back, seeking the many tributaries and, if I could, the source. And that meant moving away beyond the familiar to other times, other places. I became a nomad of the spirit, a traveller of the mind. My homeland was not a location but a route. I journeyed to America and, through poets like Whitman, Pound, Williams, Olson and Eliot, at last engaged with my European roots, which were no longer mine in particular but rather those of a community of northern poets, travellers of the mind like myself. Through all the tangled network of relations that wove the weft of northern Europe I lighted upon the long hidden yet brilliant structure of polyphonic Burgundy which I have already talked about and which seems to me a model for the Europe of the future. And from Burgundy the next thread that I followed led me, through the subtlest of routes, to the ancient culture of Ireland.

I was in Laon in Northern France situated half-way between Brussels and Paris. Laon is a citadel crowning a table of chalk rising from sea-level, the only medieval city in the region left intact after the numerous feats of destruction performed all around by generations of warring German and French armies. Laon survived because it was defeated: defeated when the Carolingian dynasty was replaced by the Paris-based Capetians. History was thenceforth closed for a town that had once been so brilliant, so renowned the world over. Laon was insulated from the depredations of history, cocooned through time, frozen (like Pompeii) in its past. Even the 1914–18 war largely passed it by; the men in their trenches and on their bellies crawling through the mud spared little thought for the citadel above. My love of Laon was aroused when I witnessed an incredibly beautiful summer sunrise hitting the Eastern rose-window of the cathedral, all the closer to the sun as it is perched atop the 'mountain'. The rose bloomed in me. I came to read about Laon and found myself pursuing several interesting clues. One concerned the etymology. 'Laon' originally comes from the same root as Lyon and perhaps London, and was first spelt Lugdunum: that is, literally, a fortress devoted to the worship of the Celtic god *Lug*, the god of Light.

Laon, from being one of the favourite cities of Charlemagne, became the capital city of his grandson Charles the Bald in the ninth century. Charles the Bald was a refined and scholarly monarch who filled his court with musicians and philosophers the stars among whom were scholars from Ireland, John Scotus Eriugena shining foremost among them. One day, I wove my way through medieval lanes with evocative names such as the rue des Irlandais to the local archive, which contains one of the richest collections of Carolingian manuscripts in existence. There I saw a copy of Eriugena's 'Commentary on the Gospel of St John', written in part in the philosopher's own hand. I saw other manuscripts in the margins of which the Irish copyists complained — in Gaelic — when the weather was too cold or the candles too low. These documents, with their so-human graffiti, were well over a thousand years old, and date from a period we deprecatingly refer to as the 'Dark Ages'. But Laon was not dark; Ireland was not dark. Is it not strange, I reflected, that those Irish monks, descendants of the early Celtic worshippers of Lug, should have come to Lug-town to start a school of philosophy known to history as the School of Light? Or had some thread of light secretly illuminated their way?

12

Towards the Light

When Irish scholars brought their 'Philosophy of Light' to Laon in northern France they also brought with them a knowledge of Greek. Absurd, in a way, that the culture of south-eastern Europe should become the special property of learned men in the north-westernmost tip. Yet there is in Laon a Greek–Latin dictionary, written by an Irishman dating from around 800 AD, which is a silent witness to a spiritual link between two fragile and far distant extremities of the Western world, Greece and Ireland, each in its day an island of scholarship, then stretching towards each other across vast expanses of space and time to meet in the tiny 'City of Light', Laon.

I wonder what the approaches to Laon would have looked like to those early Irish visitors. The city rises a sheer 300 feet above sea level and the best way to reach the summit today is by ascending a steep staircase hewn in the northern side of the hill. In June, scented roses bloom in little rock gardens on either side, and as you climb you can look back over the chequered surface of fields extending far away to the North. On emerging at the top one is struck by both the freshness and the light. Perhaps the present denizens of Laon are not quite up to the magic of the place with all its many philosophical associations; but one can easily whisk one's way back a thousand years and more through the maze of narrow medieval lanes that lie almost untouched by time.

I have a poem in *La Maye* that tries to convey my own discovery of Laon through the eyes and mind of John Scotus Eriugena. Eriugena in my poem has just completed his journey to this renowned place of learning and immediately responds to its rousing and mystical call (see *Envoi*). And how was I led to Eriugena? It was through translating the 'Cantos' of Ezra Pound. Pound in his usual elliptical way manages to drop a clue here and there concerning the great Philosopher of Light. For this I have to be immensely grateful, though Pound himself after his sojourn in northern Europe finally succumbed to the more tangible attractions of Mediterranean light which he eventually elevated to the level of a cult on his terrace at Rapallo. Pound was, and yet was not, interested in the real thing. His vision of the heavenly luminous terrace of Dioce seems to me to be derivative, to hark back too much to Flaubert's famous rendering of Carthaginian civilisation in *Salambô*. He had that late nineteenth-century habit of constant allusion: a quote here, a name dropped there, he himself a metaphor in his own writing. He coasts to Rapallo, as he had his 'Irish scholar' and friend W.B. Yeats sail to Byzantium, just to be a stone in a mosaic. You learn something of Pound from all this; but for further light on the world of Eriugena I had to search elsewhere.

James Joyce is closer to the medieval truth in a way, perhaps, when his East meets West in the double perambulation of Bloom and Dedalus. But if Yeats and Joyce saw the route, one endowed it with mystical dreams of cultural nationalism and the other made it determinedly prosaic. Neither would have been prepared to concede that there was worthy matter in the thinking of a medieval monk. Eriugena's vision of the world managed to draw both on the negative theology of the sixth-century Syrian monk Dyonysius and on the fourth-century neo-Platonism of Plotinus to present a kind of moderate rational Christianity of which poet or novelist might have approved. No; we have to part company with Pound, Joyce, Yeats and the nineteenth-century European culture that produced them, and make the journey ourselves, seeking treasures of wisdom and enlightenment that have long been disregarded both because they were written in Latin or Greek and because they presupposed Christianity. For this quest we require skills of translation and the ability to think ourselves into not only the language but the mind and spirit of others. This is the true skill of the poet.

Throughout the nineteenth century the poet was regularly conceived as a Promethean figure, stealing divine fire to pass it on to men. The poet was thus the true revolutionary, with a special line

to Hell as in the case of Baudelaire, forging fearful symmetries like
Blake, or bringing fire and steam to the people like Hugo. The
twentieth century began with a vast conflagration that none of those
had foreseen, so the 'satanic' poets were left to rake over a few
embers in a land of waste and ashes. It is time to start again. But
where? Not in a Wordsworthian retreat to hearth, home and
insularity. Not, surely, into further destructiveness, though there are
still poets who see their role as blowing on the cinders of old fires,
keeping alight forces of destruction that have almost burned
themselves out. Instead I believe a new pilgrimage awaits us as we
approach the Third Millennium: new, yet honoured by age. For the
time is here when poets should abandon fire and instead seek out
light. And in this quest John Scotus Eriugena provides a beacon and a
vision.

The vision of Eriugena is of a world in which everything ascends
to, or descends from, God. Thus, there are two kinds of light: light
proceeding from God is *lux*, and light reflected by objects back
towards God is *lumen*. Each object receives or reflects light according
to its need to be rendered understandable. In such a system faith is
never opposed to reason since God can be apprehended both
negatively (through faith) as well as positively (through science). Such
a theology of nuance and gradation allows ample space to art, to the
idea of musical scale as well as of a variegated range of shades and
colours. Indeed there must have been close contacts between
philosophers and musicians at the court of Charles the Bald in Laon
in the ninth century with results that were to have enormous
repercussions. For Charles prided himself on his support of a musical
school in Saint Amand, which produced treatises by Hucbald which
bear on the division of tones and appear to have laid the ground for
the eventual development of polyphony.

The relevance of the Philosophy of Light to our own times is more
direct than that, however. We inhabit a world where Light is a
tangible reality; *the* essential reality in a sense as it now serves as the
standard by which we measure Time as well as Space. Indeed, we
now know the two to be interdependent in a way that would have
brought a wry smile to the face of Eriugena. Two centuries ago, the
French Revolutionaries instituted the '*metre*' as the standard

measurement of space (in fact, the measurements were done by Delambre, who came from Laon!). Today the *metre* is defined not as a portion of the earth's surface, but more precisely as a fraction of the speed of light. Light is the constant that reveals the relativity of Time and Space. Light means Nature and produces the photosynthesis which renews the oxygen we need in order to survive. And light can be turned into sound by the radiotelescopes with which we scan ever more distant corners of our universe.

So we are sailing light years away from Tintern Abbey towards an ever-fleeing origin. There is no longer a golden age of mankind to be discovered somewhere in rural Cumbria or Wessex, far from the madding crowd; no virgin European nook in which to dig ourselves a fortress against the onrush of modernity. None of us is immune from the inexorable processes of history; two world wars made that brutally clear. Today, we are called upon not to retreat into the flames but to cast new light upon an ever-expanding universe of experience. The legend of Prometheus is at last replaced as, for the first time since the discovery of fire, we poets are drawn to a central metaphor which happens also to be the basis of our physical sustenance. The inner light thus meets its outer source, the planets. Poets are no longer cast as those who steal fire but as keepers and purveyors of light. This new role asks for a new art.

Thus, our voyage outwards has to begin with a journey backwards to those ages that, although less advanced technologically, were more in touch philosophically with the ether of existence. We may no longer believe in angels, but, in a way, we are closer than ever to being like them ourselves: light creatures (what a marvellous language, English, that can play on 'light' and 'lightness'!) who realise that their place is less on Earth or even under the sun than in the midst of billions of galaxies. Does this lessen the importance of mankind, or of poets in their illumination of existence? On the contrary. My feeling is that with the almost quasi-instantaneity of human messages (electronics instead of protracted letters) in the midst of our infinitely extending cosmic distances, we are on the edge of a new world which poets can help us understand, but only if they come to terms with it themselves. The instant pictures and sounds from

Neptune: these are the currency of today and if poets do not use them, others will.

Poets have not been heard in the city for some time. Perhaps it is their own fault as they imprison themselves in the incomprehensibility of their own art. They are occasionally read, but very seldom heard, except perhaps when set to other people's music. I have faith in the spoken word and believe it will be heard again. Already the great messages of the day are disseminated not principally by books, newspapers or broadsheets, but by political leaders and media personalities addressing millions of people over radio and television. We are a noisy culture, a verbal culture, a talkative culture, and tend to remember more of what we see and hear across the electronic media than of what we read. But within this chatterbox culture of instant messages, we also retain a penchant for reflection, and lend a ready ear to anyone capable of placing present preoccupations in a larger perspective. We love to hear the voices of the past and to learn of other times, other places; the places and times of our own collective birth.

Here, surely, is a new opportunity for the poet. For the poet of today, like John Scotus Eriugena in Laon all those centuries ago, has the chance and the duty to grasp the *lumen* of our perceived experience and fashion and express it in a form closer to the *lux* of its origin; to radiate in the manner of Eriugena, not to burn in the style of the followers of Prometheus, to speak lightly of light, and to ascend the hill of Lugdunum, the City of Eternal Light.

13

Beyond the Tunnel of History

The Bicentenary came and went. The various commemorations changed nothing. But how could it have been otherwise? Though it may have helped disseminate revolution all over the world, the French Revolution retains the trappings of a very local affair. Besides, was not the French Revolution responsible, to a greater or lesser degree, for such diverse offspring as the Vendée massacre, the bloodshed associated with nineteenth-century nationalism and the Bolshevik Revolution of the twentieth century? And if you *must* have a date to mark the origin of modern liberalism, is not 4 July 1776 both earlier and more appropriate than 14 July 1789?

If the Bicentenary was something of a damp squib in France itself, the most striking commemoration occurred in some of the most unexpected parts of the world. China, for example, where the occupation of Tiananmen Square in Beijing by so many students provided a perfect example of the 'democratic square' we discussd in Chapter 1. This spark of democratic freedom tragically backfired on those who had ignited it, for what was at issue was not only the growing swing towards democracy in perhaps the oldest feudal society in the world; it was also a perfect illustration of the dominance of the French Revolution in all subsequent ones, both sides in China citing French precedents for what respectively they desired and feared. All one's memories of those heady days are, however, tinged by the knowledge of the appalling brutality with which the people's revolt was finally crushed. Like Brussels, destroyed on the orders of

Louis XIV, the spirit of Tiananmen Square will surely rise again one day. But the events of 4 June 1989 reminded us, if any reminder were needed, that history works in no single 'progressivist' direction, that freedoms can be lost as well as won, and that two centuries after the American and French Revolutions the tree of liberty needs always to be watered anew.

Perhaps we should, after all, return to Europe. Even as Chinese tanks were mowing down their own citizens, the Poles were voting into power a non-Communist government and the Hungarians cutting their border fence with Austria. A few weeks later, popular pressure brought the downfall of communist power in East Germany, Czechoslovakia, Bulgaria and Romania. In Russia itself, principles were beginning to be espoused that would look moderately familiar to the ghosts of Jefferson and Mirabeau. And in Western Europe, while all those moves were being closely watched and enthusiastically applauded, history moved apace towards a single market and perhaps, in the longer run, a single Europe.

So we return where we started; to Brussels, already in so many ways *de facto* the capital of Europe, and long since at the very crossroads of cultures: English, German, French, Flemish, Spanish and Irish. This is not to say that other cities cannot claim to be in their own way the capital city of Europe. If we are to revive the medieval conception of Europe at its freest and its most open, there is room for a whole guild of cities and towns jostling and elbowing each other for temporary leadership. Movement and instability are part of the rules of the game, best reflected as we saw in that exciting modern Babel the sloping Grote Markt in Brussels itself. Western Europe cannot but thrive from the tension thus wound up between its many big cities. As London slips its moorings and rebuilds downstream, do I detect the sleepy old lion licking its chops and flexing its muscles as it glimpses the European financial markets of tomorrow?

Paris, too, is clearly limbering up to be the European capital in its own terms. Architecturally, there is probably no more beautiful city in the world, with the possible exception of New York, its more 'masculine' complement. A true European might balk at the beauty of Paris on the grounds that much of it was created from the ruins of other countries. As Louis XIV was building Versailles he was busy pounding Brussels and Heidelberg. Yet beauty constantly renewed does not necessarily imply corresponding destruction. President Mitterrand's dazzling new 'Arche de la Défense' is one of the unmitigated architectural triumphs of our time. It stands nobly along the great axis of Paris due west from the Louvre, frames the Arc de Triomphe, and manages to blend American grandeur harmoniously with European symbolism. The Cube, as Parisians have started calling it, is like a fully realised conception by Malevich. It brings back to Europe the notion of modern art that some feared had emigrated irredeemably across the Atlantic. Much of the modern arcthitecture of Europe is plateglass banal, a perfect (or grotesque) example being much that has been erected in the very area of Paris I am describing, La Défense. But the Cube itself, designed by a Dane with roots deep in European history and tradition, does not merely proclaim its own grandeur at the expense of the little people around it like so much American architecture. Here, the grandeur retains its humanity, taking inspiration from the past (the Arc de Triomphe, the Concorde, the Louvre, the Bastille, Vincennes) as well as from contemporary and futuristic models.

Time will tell whether the Arche eventually supplants that old logo of Paris on stamps and souvenirs, the original Iron Lady, the Eiffel Tower. Meanwhile, I like to see in the Arche de la Défense and in some of the other spectacular recent architectural additions to our Parisian landscape a symbol of something deeper, a shift in French attitudes less concrete than the erection of new buildings, yet more significant. The architect of the Arche is a Dane; the Pyramid at the Louvre was designed by a Chinese-American, the Pompidou Centre by an Englishman and an Italian. There are, of course, plenty of excellent French architects and they have been responsible for much outstanding work. But I seem to detect the germs of a new cosmopolitanism in French cultural life, an openness to creative impulses whatever their provenance that is in stark and refreshing contrast to our accustomed intellectual chauvinism.

This does not mean abandoning the past. No architecture taking its inspiration from Roman triumphal arches or Egyptian pyramids could be accused of that. On the contrary, it means drawing sustenance from sources more widely and securely spread. The old-fashioned celebration of French nationalism fails to ignite the fancy as it used to do: do you recall the almost whimsical absurdity of our Bicentennial marchpast? And in Lille and Nancy, Lyon, Montpellier and Toulouse, a new spirit of international entrepeneurship is awakening in excited response to a world of the TGV (bullet train), fax, minitel and satellite television. The youngsters are learning to speak (and eat) like their neighbours in Germany, Italy or Spain. And everywhere people are learning English, which is thought to provide a passport to American know-how and British culture. For all the superficial animosity that remains between France and England, the inevitable vestige of hundreds of years of war, I think I detect a new *mutualité*, a profound sense of siblings outgrowing the destructive rivalries of childhood and striving to achieve a genuinely harmonious maturity.

This may all be wishful thinking, a dream on my part. The rhetoric of French nationalism still rings through the air and, on the political right, has millions of fervent adherents. It is still *lèse-majesté* in some quarters to praise Shakespeare over Racine (just as it was for Berlioz over a century ago) even though – possibly *because* – Shakespeare palpably led English culture to a far wider universality than our French classicism was ever to do.

Present dreams, however, can help nourish a future reality, working below the surface like those who are building that most tangible yet invisible symbol of the new spirit of *mutualité*, the Channel Tunnel. The Tunnel has, in a sense, been many hundreds of years in the making; a profound – literally subterranean – force of history working away against the tide of nationalism that has periodically risen and ebbed on either shore. Tunnels run in two directions, towards the future and the past, and the Channel Tunnel will be no exception. It will obviously have major implications for the future of both Britain and France and indeed elsewhere in Europe. Trade, travel, tourism and the rest will all be radically affected. But so will our view of the past. Perhaps we will at last learn that nationalism was a recent invention that cannot sensibly be read back into British and French history more than a mere handful of centuries, and that the most valuable legacies of the past have been bequeathed by those cultures most open to enrichment from external influences. It is the universality of Shakespeare, not his nationalism, that elevates him above his contemporaries, the humanity of Mozart and not the technical facility of his writing, the shared intimacies of Bruegel not his draftsmanship, the polyphony of Josquin and the integrated versatility of Erasmus or Leonardo for which we venerate these men of genius. As we French or British tunnel our way through the subterranean rocks of our respective histories, we must hope to emerge into a new Lugdunum, a new City of Light, a new and successful Babel of tongues and cultures jostling together to the mutual enrichment of all.

I will certainly want to be there. Perhaps I am already, for I have long felt myself to be almost an Englishman in the French language just as some English authors aspire to write in their own language with the limpidity of French. And as for that subterranean, subconscious cross-Channel Tunnel, this is something I passed through long ago. In a way, my own career has paralleled (I even like to think prefigured) some of the wider developments I see around me. As I return once more to my childhood home in the Forest of Crécy, and to my faithful little river, the Maye, I know that when the time comes I will be among the first to travel through the new Tunnel, the first to exult in the new Grote Market of Europe and to celebrate a renewed Fête de la Fédération, proud to play my part in the greatest authentic polycentric culture since medieval Burgundy while still retaining my roots deep in the soil of northern France.

John Scotus Eriugena in Laon

It is an Ireland of chalk,
with the sky for a sea,
the beach all over blue, the green
of vines scooped in a ring,

in a creek where subtle waves of lapping air
make the eyes bob like boats
come from the ocean and the *viator*,
standing up, would seem about

to step ashore, the deeps of air
elude his grasp, he swings round,

his eyes beholding hold wavers
at an angle, his stand on the ground
shakes, his head of a sudden
is tossed sheer of the rock

abruptly straining his gaze, drowning
him in fire, he flares up,
like a piece of smooth silk
lit by a cinder, he burns

and does that mean that Hell is blue,
and does that mean the sun is God's reverse?

This is a Northern Lugdunum
where he lands, the white *arx* of Laon,
fortress of chalk once used by Gauls
as a temple to Lug, their god

their divine head of Light,
and he, Hibernian Celt,
putting his feet on that podium
that *puy*, floating platform

at clouds' and winds' level
that blow wide from the North Pole,

inhales the quintessence of rain,
the heather-rose tones
of altitude, the water turned
to snow at the first sign of cold.

Fire pours. The pure light of autumn
blanches the hill, the tufa
echoes the light, one might see
stray off its moorings far north

into the plains, a Greek Cyclade
sprung up from a mistranslation.

From Lindisfarne, let us assume —
even though Albinus through his letters
to the monks of the island exhorting them
to fend off the Vikings might prove

a counter-evidence – it was his reading Greek,
which made Carolus Calvus, that offshoot
from the Mosan stock of Pippinides
call him to his side, in Laon,

to translate Dionysius. Rustling through
the king's vineyards and the blue sky

comes the soughing sound of the North Sea
through the Holy Island straits
when the flow ebbs in and the seals
bark, Johannes from Hibernia

listens, his Latin curragh,
which he deems far too gross for steering
by Greek headlands, carries along
the wafting sound from the long rolling surf

of Scotland, a scent of wrack *where like
unto an amber stone nests the halcyon.*

The unattainable might well have the look
of the stone he has just landed on,
that chalk which is both gloom
and whiteness, blindly he climbs

the sun tilts up, he falls
from as high as he has ascended, would Satan,
between his eyes welcome as candidly
the dark stone light,

would he, as totally, the fine scent
of peppered roses stinging his senses

from each side of the stairs?
The sky is made purer by air,
it is to calculate the distance
from thing to thing that he ascends, that he

descends, the world divisions
tighten up, light up between the lines,
the untouchable frontier assumes
luminous shades, the opacity

of the grain shines, the sun bites
at the edges of reality, the image dies.

Dionysius, founding father of cathedrals
to come, tutor of naves, of window
roses, whose spider-web of shades
captures daylight at dawn

in the East, Ionian Lord,
Lord of Eastern Ionas, Dionysius,
on thy Lugdunum hill
your Greek wanders, your darkness rains

its *alphs*, its alphas, the morning wealth
starts pouring its *dations*.

John Scot comments, his violet ink
stirs up Plato's igneous creation,
sifts through the enmeshed eye
a husky flour, the bran of light

clogs the fine sieves
that part theology, while in the cave
where the shadows are, the natives
make fire from any wood,

hoc lignum, make light
from any common stone, *lapis iste.*

And if, should ask some clown,
Quomodo omnia, quae sunt,
Lumina sunt? the pedagogue
picks up a stone, a slate

from the very vineyard of Laon, plainly
plying his learning to the fractal
matter that he crumbles, a honeycomb
in the blue buzzing sky

all around, the clarity, the sapidity,
the unctuous contact with the stone

rouses the right idea
whose line recoups another one,
degrees are hewn, cross each other,
from the taut stone

rears up a temple, attention fans
a whole scale of effects, smooths
the planes, welcomes praying
into itself through increase

in volume of silence that spreads
from the vaulted pointed edges.

See! he holds Ireland in his hand
as did Carolus Magnus the imperial
apple topped with the cross.
To ward off idolatry

should consist first in compacting
divine Earth together, in hardening
its kernel, its core, its radiant
blindness to light, its *tenebra*

according to Dionysius, and then
hurling up into the sky that

fistful of stars for it to flame up
like a ball of sun, like a cormorant, like a dark
pennon, for its vinery of chalk
to crack in the blue veins of *Ouranos*,

the limpid vault will take it
as a ripe cherry cascading from the leaves
of a cherry-tree, in June, down the bars
of the ladder, when thrown from so far

away the Earth is but a fruity seed
in God's fleshy season.

In the vats at Laon the light
squelches from under the treader's feet,
the Grecian hill bleeds its light wine
clearer than juice from Santorin,

the funnel tilts back, blue
overflows, the world in spate
protects him from drowning, God
has created as many things as

are in his glory, *hilaritas!* joy will
night on the hill, the winter

of objects recedes into He from whom
they luminously proceed, and we
walking philosophers, walkers
through *photodosia*, ascend

the steps of the world inasmuch
as it suits us to climb,
Earth in one hand, one knee on earth,
our pilgrimage to humbleness,

our hilarious journey to the hill
of Time, the hill at Laon.

(Translated by Jacques Darras,
 with help from Ruth Fainlight)

Jean Scot Erigène à Laon

C'est une Irlande de craie, la mer
serait figurée par le ciel,
la plage partout est bleue, le vert
des vignes est arrondi en cirque,

en crique où clapote l'air subtil
dans lequel dansent les yeux, comme barques
venant du large, et le *viator*,
debout sur ses jambes se préparerait

à débarquer, le fond de l'air
le fuit, se dérobe, le ballotte

le secoue sur sa prise d'angle
avec les yeux, l'assise soudain
du monde chavire, et voici que
sa tête culbutant à l'abrupt

de la roche, violemment lui tourne
le regard, le noie dans du feu,
il s'enflamme, claque comme une soie
fine qu'une braise aurait allumée

il brûle, l'Enfer serait-il bleu,
l'envers de Dieu est-ce le soleil?

Il est à Laon, la Lugdunum
du Nord; la crayeuse citadelle
où il aborde, *arx* blanche, naguère
fut le temple du dieu Lug, gaulois,

divinité de la lumière,
et lui, le Celte d'Hibernie
posant le pied sur ce *podium*,
ce puy, cette plate-forme flottant

à hauteur de nuages, de vents
soufflant du large septentrion,

hume la quintessence des pluies,
l'altitude presque égale au rose
de la bruyère, l'eau qui se
change en neige aux tous premiers froids.

Il tombe du feu. La pure lumière
d'automne blanchit le mont, le tuf
reverbère l'éclat, on dirait
d'une Cyclade égarée, très haut,

dans les plaines, île hellène jaillie
d'un contre-sens de traduction.

A Lindisfarne, nous supposerons –
même si Alcuin par ses missives
aux moines de l'île les exhortant
à combattre le *Viking* est une

contre-évidence – qu'il étudia
le Grec, que Carolus Calvus,
du cep mosan des Pippinides
l'appela auprès de lui, à Laon,

pour y traduire Denys. Entre
les vignes royales et le ciel bleu

se glisse un bruit de mer du Nord
au goulet de l'Ile Sainte quand le
jusant reflue et que les phoques
aboient, Johannes l'Hibernien

l'écoute, son coracle latin,
qu'il juge trop fruste pour son périple
aux presqu'îles du grec, emporte
un friselis des houles longues

d'Ecosse, une saveur d'algues où niche
ainsi qu'un joyau d'ambre l'halcyon.

L'inaccessible aurait figure
de cette roche qu'il vient d'aborder,
comme un craie ténébreuse et blanche
à la fois, aveugle il gravit

la pente, le soleil penche, il tombe
d'aussi haut qu'il gravit, Satan
accueillerait-il l'obscur éclat
de pierre entre ses yeux, comme lui,

et la pointe finement poivrée des roses
qui aiguillent ses sens de chaque

côté des marches, d'une aussi pure
candeur? L'air raréfie le ciel,
c'est pour *calculer* la distance
entre les choses qu'il monte, ou qu'il

descend, la division du monde
se tend, s'éclaire entre les lignes,
l'impalpable frontière se bistre
d'ombre lumineuse, l'opacité

du grain rayonne, le soleil mord
aux marges du réel, l'image meurt.

Denys, le socle des cathédrales
à venir, tuteur des nefs, des
roses vitrail, arachnées d'ombres
à capturer le jour vers l'Est,

quand il point, Seigneur d'Ionie,
d'Ionas orientale, Denys,
sur la colline lugdunienne
ton grec navigue, ta ténèbre pleut

se alphas, ses alphées, l'aube
entame l'abondance de ses dations.

Jean Scot commente, son encre violette
rallume, ignée, la création
platonicienne, tamise au rets
de l'œil une fleur grumeleuse

le son, le bran de la lumière
corrompt la finesse des blutages
théologiques, dans la caverne
aux ombres les indigènes font feu

de tout bois *hoc lignum,* lueur
des pierres communes, *lapis iste.*

Et si, demande quelque rustaud,
Quomodo omnia, quae sunt,
lumina sunt? le pédagogue
ramasse un caillou, une roche

à même la vigne de Laon, applique
son savoir simple à la matière
anfractueuse, l'effrite, gâteau
de miel au bourdonnement du bleu

du ciel alentour, la clarté,
la saveur, le toucher onctueux

de la pierre suscitent l'idée juste
dont la ligne recoupe une autre
idée, les marches se taillent, se croisent,
du caillou naît un temple qui vibre

en ses tensions, l'attention creuse
une hiérarchie d'effets, polit
les plans, accueille la prière
en son sein par l'accroissement

du volume du silence qui sourd
à l'ogive des arêtes, des angles.

Il tient l'Irlande dans sa main
comme Carolus Magnus la pomme
d'Empire surmontée de la croix.
Mettre à distance l'idolâtrie

consiste d'abord à rassembler
la Terre divinement, en durcir
le noyau, le cœur, l'aveugle
cécité solaire, la ténèbre

selon Denys, puis dépêcher
au ciel la poignée astrale, pour

qu'elle s'illumine boule de soleil,
oiseau cormorant, oriflamme
noire, qu'elle crépite crayeuse vinière
aux veines bleues d'*Ouranos*, la voûte

limpide l'accueillera dans son sac
comme cerise mûre qui tombe des feuilles
du cerisier, en Juin, aux barres
de l'échelle, jetée d'aussi loin

la Terre n'est plus que graine fruitière
en la pulpeuse saison de Dieu.

Aux fouloirs, à Laon, la lumière
gicle sous les pieds du marcheur, la
colline grecque saigne d'un vin léger
plus clair que jus de Santorin,

l'entonnoir se renverse, du bleu
déborde, la crue du monde le sauve
de son engloutissement, Dieu a
créé autant de choses qu'il a

de gloire, *hilaritas!* la joie
s'anuite sur le mont, l'hiver

des choses récède en Dieu dont elles
procèdent lumineusement, et nous
philosophes de la marche, marcheurs
de la *photodosie,* allons

aux degrés du monde autant qu'il
nous plaît de faire son ascension,
Terre dans une main, genou en Terre,
pélerinage d'humilité,

voyage d'hilarité à la
montagne de Laon, montagne du Temps.